Living the Life-Force

...and Finding Your Own Way to Do It

By
Nicholas Vesey

For permission, serialization, condensation, adaptions, or for our catalog of other publications, write to Ozark Mountain Publishing, Inc., P.O. Box 754, Huntsville, AR 72740, ATTN: Permissions Department.

Library of Congress Cataloging-in-Publication Data

Vesey, Nicholas – 1954 -
Living the Life-Force by Nicholas Vesey

This book is a 'primer' on spirituality for those reluctant to join anything.

1. Enlightenment 2. Spirituality 3.Consciousness 4. Metaphysical
I. Vesey, Nicholas, 1954 - II. Metaphysical   III.. Spirituality IV. Title

Library of Congress Catalog Card Number:2019933012
ISBN: 9781940265612

Cover Art and Layout: Victoria Cooper Art
Book set in: Times New Roman, Gabriola
Book Design: Tab Pillar
Published by:

PO Box 754, Huntsville, AR 72740
800-935-0045 or 479-738-2348; fax 479-738-2448
WWW.OZARKMT.COM

Printed in the United States of America

For Heather, Samuel, and Jessica.
The family I always wanted.

Contents

Introduction

What do we know?

We pretend we know what is going on in life, but often we haven't a clue. We put on our "game faces" and hope that no one is going to see that really we are out of control. We might be able to get from A to B, to put our trousers on the right way, and make some sort of show of capability at work, on the yoga mat, or as we steer our kids through life; but look beneath the surface, and most of us are just "winging it" to a greater or lesser degree. We just don't want to get found out. Where exactly that competence ends and the winging it begins depends on the individual.

To some of us raising children is a complete mystery; we do what we can, and we just hope no one really looks too hard and suggests that "We need to talk about Kevin." Others can get the job done, but when pressed as to why we have ended up doing the job, where it is going to lead, and how we feel about it in the scheme of things, well, we would prefer not to be pressed. And then there is the "I haven't a clue, and hope I don't have to explain" level. That includes questions like, What happens when we die? Where did we come from? What is time? What is consciousness? And what do we do about gun laws?

The point where we move from competency to cluelessness really depends upon how honest we are and what we choose to believe in. An atheist will pretty quickly get to not knowing what happens after we die, an agnostic will want to hedge their bets, and a fully paid-up member of many religions will want to go into a lot of detail. We tend to avoid looking at exactly where we will admit to not knowing, because culturally "not to know" is seen as weakness. We just keep our shit together as long as possible, and then when the moment comes when the shit will not be kept together any longer, we finally hold our hands up to the reality that we are now well and truly full of whatever waste material we have been carrying. It is one of the great unwritten commandments that "Thou shalt not be found out as being stupid," and to admit to "not knowing" is tantamount to admitting the worst.

But there is, surprisingly, quite a bit that we do not know. We do not know how our hearts beat, how we breathe, how we think, what it is that is thinking, if the brain makes thought, or if thought makes the brain, what is going to happen next, what just happened, how it all works, and who the fuck is in charge anyway. To begin to admit to all this seems like the road to insanity, but it is in reality the road to … well, we do not know that either, but it is more on the sane side than the insane side.

Then there is the whole question as to why we are here anyway. Is it to help corporations make profits? Is it to add more children into the world? Is it to fight for the previous generation's values and ideas? It is another "who knows?" But we all have a purpose in life. Even if we are unaware of that purpose, or cannot vocalize it, it exists. We all do things for a reason. Your purpose is a function of perspective. Get the wrong perspective, and you end up with the wrong purpose or not so much the wrong purpose, as the right purpose for the wrong perspective.

And yet, even that is not quite right, because how can you have a wrong perspective? It is just your perspective, right or wrong. But your perspective is certainly key to what your life is about. When your perspective is that your house is on fire, then your purpose is to put it out. When you see that your house is on fire because we are under attack from aliens and the world is about to come to an end, then fuck your house, there is a bigger game in play. Size matters. The bigger your perspective, the more you can get a handle as to what is really going on in life, and act accordingly. A meth addict is all about getting more meth. A concerned parent is about looking after their kids. And a corporate CEO has whatever perspective corporate CEOs have. Each has a different purpose in life, and each acts out his or her life accordingly.

This book is about exploring the nature of perspective.

I am going to suggest that it is possible to have a perspective that includes all life as we know it, and some that we do not. Having such a perspective enables us to act in a way that is appropriate not only to ourselves, but also to our families, our friends, all of humanity, and the planet itself. This perspective includes the whole universe, both known and unknown. And in acting out of that perspective, I want to suggest that we are able to have a positive effect on everything.

I do not propose to offer any "proofs" for the ideas that I am putting down here; I am just asking you to consider them as ideas. Do they ring true for you? Could they be true? And if they were true, what effect might they have on the way that you live your life? I do not know if I am right in what I am saying here; in fact, I offer this book with the willingness to be wrong. You be the judge. The ideas come from a distillation of forty years of being on this path, a path that is trying to work out what the fuck is going on in life. Where does it all come from? What does it all mean? Is there such a thing or person as God? Is there any order in the universe? If there is, how do we recognize it?

Living the Life-Force is to me the ultimate challenge. Is there a Life-Force we can tap into, and if so, what part do we have to play in all of it?

All the time we are trying to get it right: to eat the right food, to do the right yoga, to get the right job, to meet the right person, to bring up our children right, to generally live right. What does it mean to live right? Does it mean to copy others that we feel have lived right? Do we try and work it all out and come up with a way of right living? Or is there something intrinsic that we can tap into that will show us what to do? That is what this book is about; and it is not so much me telling you what is so, as me suggesting some ideas and you seeing what is true for you.

If you have read this far down the page, then we are probably in the same game and it is worth reading on, because this affects everything we do at every moment of our day. We make a decision to exercise or to have a cup of coffee. To read a book or to watch a film. To go out or to stay in. At every moment we are faced with forks in the road, and decisions as to which path to take. The big question is, on what basis do we make those decisions? Do we make them unconsciously, or are we deliberate? How do we decide, and from what perspective? We consider these things when we are faced with the big decisions in life, but in a way it is the little decisions that lead us to the point where we have to make the big decisions.

There is a story of a married couple celebrating their golden wedding anniversary, and the husband gets up to make a speech. "When we got married my wife and I decided that I would make all the really important decisions in life, and she would make all the less important ones. It just so happens that in fifty years of marriage there were never any really important decisions that needed to be made."

Life is all about those small seemingly unimportant decisions. Turn left here, turn right here until eventually we come to a point where we are faced with the consequences of those supposedly unimportant decisions. On what basis do we decide? What is our perspective and what is our purpose?

That is what we are exploring here.

Part 1
In Theory

Chapter 1
WTF Is Going On?

What can you rely on?

Some things we take for granted—the sun comes up every day, rocks are hard, and water is wet. But beyond that we live day to day with uncertainty. The sun may rise in the morning, but there is no guarantee that we will have our health, or wealth, or family, or our position in life. We know there is order in life, because the earth goes around the sun every day and our ass points downward, but does that mean that I can rely on meeting the man or woman of my dreams, or that the stock market will continue to rise? Certainly not. It does not seem that this order extends into our personal lives.

If you are of a religious bent you can start to talk about karma or God, but then we are straying into territory that has been fought over for years and to which there is no simple answer. There is no benefit in having a universe that is ordered and has certainty if that certainty ends at our personal life. It seems that we can predict almost anything except the thing that is really important—what is going to happen to us and what should we do about it.

There is an apocryphal story about Albert Einstein. Even if he never said it, it is worth reading anyway.

> When he first arrived in America he was asked by a reporter: "What, in your opinion is the most important question facing humanity today?"
>
> Einstein replied, "The most important question facing humanity is, 'Is the universe a friendly place?' This is the first and most basic question all people must answer for themselves.
>
> "For if we decide that the universe is an unfriendly place, then we will use our technology, our scientific discoveries and our natural resources to achieve safety and power by creating bigger walls to keep out the unfriendliness and bigger weapons to destroy

3

all that which is unfriendly and I believe that we are getting to a place where technology is powerful enough that we may either completely isolate or destroy ourselves as well in this process.

"If we decide that the universe is neither friendly nor unfriendly and that God is essentially 'playing dice with the universe,' then we are simply victims to the random toss of the dice and our lives have no real purpose or meaning.

"But if we decide that the universe is a friendly place, then we will use all our technology, our scientific discoveries and our natural resources to create tools and models for understanding that universe. Because power and safety will come through understanding its workings and its motives."[1]

And that really sums up our dilemma. Is the universe friendly to us or not? The word *friend* comes from the Proto-Germanic word *frijand*, which means lover. So, the question here is about whether the universe actually loves us or not. And most of the time the answer to that question is "not." For example, when we lose all our money or our health, when our partner leaves us, or when a child dies, we rage against this so-called friendly universe, and we are quite clear that it does not love us. That is our perspective, and we are sticking to it.

But, seen from outer space, the loss of our partner or the collapse of our finances is nothing. Not even a blip. It is our perspective that makes us feel unloved. If we had a different perspective, would that alter the experience we have of life? It all comes down to the nature of order and our place within that order.

The Nature of Order

The Old English definition of order is "a system of parts subject to certain uniform, established ranks or proportions." The problem is that most of the time we do not experience order. We experience life as chaos: the chaos of life, the chaos of nature, the chaos of the weather, the chaos of war; the randomness of terrorism, crime, health, finance, and the market. The smart money out there is on the fact that we live in a chaotic world with no order.

Well, on one level there is obviously order. The ceiling is not falling in, yet. The earth continues to revolve. The planets take up their appointed places in the universe. And from a distance it all looks rosy in the garden. But our experience is very different. And that is because there is chaos out there. In Tennyson's poem "In Memoriam," he talks of Nature, red in tooth and claw:

> Who trusted God was love indeed
> And love Creation's final law—
> Tho' Nature, red in tooth and claw
> With ravine, shriek'd against his creed—
>
> ....
>
> O life as futile, then, as frail!
> O for thy voice to soothe and bless!
> What hope of answer, or redress?
> Behind the veil, behind the veil.[2]

We know that chaos—we live it daily, so how can we say that there is order in life? Where is the veil to draw back into order?

"O life as futile then as frail." "What hope of answer, or redress?" That is our experience we feel nature red in tooth and claw; we know that we cannot control it; and any attempt to control it causes pain and madness. Look at Howard Hughes padding around his apartment on Kleenexes trying to avoid germs, with all the money in the world, and brought down by bugs. So how do we square the order in the universe with the chaos that so often appears in our lives?

We have to begin by looking at where that chaos is actually experienced—in our minds. The chaos we see "out there" is mirrored by the chaos within that tries to make sense of it. Our thoughts run around trying to find ways of getting in control. And so one place where we can begin to create order from this disorder is to discipline our minds. We start with the one place we can have an effect on— that which is within us, our minds.

When we begin to discipline our thinking we bring order to one of the parts of the chaos that is happening in our lives. And our mind is the one place where we can exert order.

Using techniques like mindfulness, yoga, and meditation, we can exert some kind of control and this allows us to separate ourselves from the experience of chaos that we face most of the time.

Without the quietening of the mind, we ourselves become a part of the chaos. We are thrown about by all the chaotic human behavior that we see around us. At some point we have to put a stop to the way we react, and the first port of call is our minds.

To let ourselves be affected by the chaos in the world without controlling our reactions is to allow ourselves to become amplifiers of that chaos. The alternative is to try to make sense of the chaos. To search for the order that is within it. People often try to see God's good and perfect plans in the unfolding of life.

They try to see that order in terms of both good and evil. They point to God in the heavens, to Jesus, to the saints, and they say, look, it is ordered, be good and God will love you. Obey the law and all will be OK; and then you get cancer, or are robbed. Because order does not work like that. The order is not "out there." You are just joining up the dots with wishful thinking. This is when religion becomes an idealized fabricated reality that we try and live within, until we cannot.

So how do we find that order? We can discipline our minds and experience a calmness within, but does that give any reality to there being an order within?

T. S. Eliot suggests where that order might be in the *Four Quartets*:

> At the still point of the turning world.
> Neither flesh nor fleshless;
> Neither from nor towards; at the still point,
> there the dance is,
> But neither arrest nor movement.
> And do not call it fixity,
> Where past and future are gathered.
> Neither movement from nor towards,
> Neither ascent nor decline.
> Except for the point, the still point,
> There would be no dance, and there is only the dance.[3]

He is saying that there is a still point within us that points to a fundamental order. And if it exists, he is suggesting that our role is to embody it; to bring order out of the chaos by touching that still point in the turning world within us. To become that "still point": in our relationships, in our finances, in the way we live, in our houses, in our bodies, in the earth. To bring order into our lives and confront the chaos we find from within, we find a sacred space within ourselves that cannot be touched by the chaos that is outside.

To have things neat and tidy is not about control. If you are sane you will know that control is impossible. Instead we seek an expression of order that welcomes chaos when it comes and always responds with an understanding that the chaos is a part of a greater order that we can see through the eye of our deeper experience. We embody rather than suppress. We trust rather than fear, we love rather than blame, surrender rather than impose. We are not attached to the outcome.

The Culture of Order

The predominant thrust of our different world cultures has not been to go within to find a place of peace within the chaos, but rather to explain the chaos.

From whatever culture we come from, we tell the story of order from our own perspective. To that end, religion is often a cultural interpretation of the nature of order—seen from its own perspective. Christians see order from the Christian perspective, mediated through Jesus's experience of the nature of reality and how he and his followers interpreted that. Buddhists do the same with the Buddha's experience. Muslims see their reality through the lens of Mohammed, and so on. Each culture defines its understanding of order through the perspective of the insight of a founder and the interpretation of that insight by the founder and followers. So the religion gives a context of order of the experience of chaos. Christians might say that the world is in chaos because of original sin, Buddhists might put it down to the four noble truths and the nature of suffering, and so on.

Whether we are Muslim, Christian, Buddhist, Jew, or atheist, each of us also has our own religion: the way that we individually interpret the experience of the culture within which we exist. We take these meta-narratives and spin our own micro-narrative, that tells us how the death of our spouse fits into that narrative, or our failing health, or the existence of war. Or not. We explain our lives through the stories we tell ourselves. But when these idealized fabricated realities fail to conform to the way our life turns out, through, for example, the death of a loved one or the loss of health or wealth, then we can "lose our faith" in our stories and re-appraise our worldview. We spin our own religion around the religion that we have been spun, and therefore make sense of the world. We all make sense of the order of the cosmos in our own way, and, as such, create our own realities.

The science fiction writer Philip K. Dick once described reality as "That which continues to exist after you've stopped believing in it."[4] And to that end, our journey here is to work out what is real, and what is made up.

Life-Force?

The key to this is trying to work out if there is an ultimate Life-Force behind everything. We might not immediately be able to talk about that in terms of a God or some form of intelligent design, but the fact that life goes on in the way that it does suggests that there is some impulse that we are a part of.

We do nothing to bring ourselves into being, and yet here we are. Yes, our parents had something to do with that; however, the sheer force of history tells us that something is unfolding. Big bang, planets, life, us. There is your order that keeps everything going, an imperative toward life that you could call a "Life-Force." But once again the question is really how deep that Life-Force reaches. Does it run into our individual lives or not? Does it affect the way we experience our lives; does it touch our individual stories? If it does, then the order that we are a part of is that Life-Force. Our very lives are an expression of it. But that is quite a leap to make. It is one thing to say that there is a force that keeps life going, but another to suggest that it actually cares about each of us as individuals. That it is not just a material disinterested order, Einstein's middle way, but an order that we are intimately involved with, that somehow is a part of who we are; and that shifts the emphasis from order to something more personal.

How do we bridge that gap between Richard Dawkins's selfish gene and the idea of a loving force that we can become intimately involved with? The latter suggests something that consciously cares about us in a way that we consciously care about others. It has a quality of nurture about it that we are involved in. In short, is there such a thing as a caring being, force, or person, that which is traditionally called "God?"

And, of course, people have been trying to prove whether or not God does exist for centuries, and the smart money is on the fact that you cannot prove whether there is intelligent design or not.

Who knows who or what "God" is? It seems to me highly arrogant for us to think we can conceive the nature of that which made us. Like ants trying to understand a human being from the sole of his or her foot. We surely cannot presume to be able to comprehend so vast an idea as our creator; and yet we can acknowledge the possibility of design. There does seem to be latent potential expressing itself in the history of evolution as it moves onward from species to species showing greater complexity and greater facility. Now that may all be coincidence or happenstance, but there is the possibility that there could be some design.

But How Do You Prove That Intelligent Design Exists?

People have always struggled and failed to prove that God does exist. If the idea of some sort of ordering function is beyond space and time, you cannot measure it, and if you cannot measure it, how do you know that it exists? Since the enlightenment, proof of something has always been about repeated measurement demonstrating the efficacy of a theory. That is, until quantum physics came along, and then what was previously merely objective became subjective.

Quantum physics came about when scientists could not explain the placing of electrons during various experiments, until finally they realized that the thing that was making the difference was the presence of the observer. The very fact of observing something affected the outcome. It started the idea that reality could be expressed in terms of relationship. So the idea of trying to prove that there is such a thing as intelligent design can be seen not only as a function of objective proof, but also in terms of relationship.

When we try to prove the existence of this "intelligent design," looking at the material side of life, we can prove nothing. But when we include ourselves in the picture we can focus on a different perspective, our own experience.

That opens up a whole new area of evidence that has previously been dismissed as objective. Experiences of love and beauty and wonder. Things that seem to transcend the rational, but are still very real.

I would like to suggest that the nearest we can come to proving the existence of this intelligent design is when our experience tells us something that the material universe does not. We can often have an experience of peace, or love, or bliss, or joy in the face of circumstances that simply do not warrant these experiences. You hear of people in extreme situations who nevertheless are at peace.

I would like to suggest that this experience of unwarranted peace is kind of a proof, as are the irrational experiences of love, beauty, and wonder. The very fact that we have these irrational notions points us to some deeper order that cannot be empirically proved.

These experiences have touched people in many different circumstances in life, and with these experiences comes a kind of certainty about life. We are touched by something that is not from "out there," but from within. It is not a mist that descends on us, but it comes from our center, and it gives us a peace that cannot be explained.

I am not just talking about a rational "being at peace"; I am referring to something deeper, something of our soul that says to us that all will be well, when often it looks like all will not be well. I think this is the nearest we can come to knowing whether this Life-Force exists or not. At this stage, all we can do is include the possibility of there being something more, but not knowing what that more might be.

Such experiences challenge us to reflect on the natural order and ask how we can cooperate with it in such a way as to manifest wholeness in our life. What can we do to bring about the greatest good? More importantly, how must we be in our lives?

The Nature of Being

"Being" is a very elusive topic. The moment you think about it, you are not actually "being" but thinking, and so you have lost it before you even start. But we talk about it a lot.

There was a time when it was fashionable to go into the whole "Be, Do, Have" thing. Be a healthy person. Do all the things that healthy people do and you will have health: "Be" a rich person, "do" all the things that rich people do, and you will "have" riches.

We think a lot about what we do. Often, in difficult situations we wring our hands and say, "What can I do? I have to *do* something." We judge people by what they do: "he does a lot of charity work"; "she was at Standing Rock"; "we went on that demonstration." We prize what people do. We like to see results. It is not enough for people just to "be"; they have to get things done.

Also, the idea of "being" does not always imply "good," although we often think so: "If only I could just 'be,' we say, 'just be in the moment.'"

But "being" is not necessarily a good thing. We talk about people "being" a pain. You can be "pure evil." You can "be" anything. The nature of being is really the essence of what you choose to operate out of. There is an aspect of it that is uncalculated. Or rather it is calculated, but that calculation has already been made instantly within us, and we operate out of the results of that calculation. As we live our lives we grow up making decisions about the way that life is. These decisions may or may not be correct, but they result in a "worldview." We settle on an idea of the way the world is, and then operate out of that. Whether that is decided through nature or nurture, a decision is made. This worldview might say that "everyone is mean and out for their own ends," or it might be that "there is a fundamental interconnectedness of all things," and that "the universe is a friendly place." Whatever our worldview, it will affect the way that we are—or how we are being. These are the decisions we default to when we think about things.

That is why some people end up being a pain, or being evil, or being good. So, when you think about the nature of your being—which of course you should not, because then you are really thinking rather than being—when you think about the nature of your being, you have to look at the worldview that you come from. You have to be aware of the beliefs and assumptions that run you when you choose to run on automatic. This means there is no intrinsic good in pure "being"; there is just a series of assumptions that we come from without thinking about them.

Developing Worldviews

Our worldviews affect the way that we think, so it is important to have some idea of the worldview that we come from. This could be anything. It all depends on what decisions we have made about the way that life is. However, there has been quite a lot of work done on the different stages of consciousness that many of us go through as we progress through our lives. Don Beck has developed some of these ideas in his Spiral Dynamics theory, and if you want to read more I would recommend Ken Wilber's *A Theory of Everything* or Jim Marion's *Putting on the Mind of Christ*.

From this work, I have drawn out six levels of consciousness to highlight. They show how our thinking develops as we develop, and also how culture expresses itself through these six levels. In the second half of this book I have looked at my own life journey through the prism of each of these levels. In looking at how we live, we might sometimes be aware of what we are thinking (mindfulness), but not be aware of the underlying framework behind our thinking, the assumptions that we make behind every thought. These stages of consciousness go some way to explain how our thinking develops.

Generally, the story of the development of these worldviews is really the story of decreasing narcissism. The dictionary definition of narcissism is "an excessive interest in one's own self, importance, and abilities." As we develop, we tend to become less fascinated with ourselves and more fascinated with others. A young child is totally egocentric in that he cannot even differentiate himself from the rest of the world. When he plays hide and seek he will hide in the broad view of others. He feels that his pain is the world's pain. He cannot differentiate between himself and the world. But as we develop, we learn that there is another world out there, and we learn how to interact with it. These different levels of consciousness show how we develop as we interact with the world and how we gradually increase our ability to cooperate with the universe that is around us.

The Levels of Consciousness

All of us travel through these levels in our lives. Each level of consciousness tends to be less egocentric than the previous one. However, it is not a straight line from one to the other. Some of us get stuck in different levels, and we can move in and out of these levels as we interact with different aspects of our lives. In that sense, we cannot see one level as bad and another as good. We travel through them all; and interestingly enough, each level of consciousness also has a parallel in the way we have developed as a culture. You can see these levels of consciousness manifesting in the different ways people behave in society.

Infant Consciousness

This is the first level of consciousness and it is predominately impulsive in character. It relates to the first stages of life. Freud called it "Primary Narcissism"—original self-centeredness: The child and the mother are one and there is total dependence. The age is from birth to two years. At this level, we are mainly concerned with me and mine. What I can get for me and what is mine. It is about satisfying our basic needs. In order to progress, the infant has to both differentiate from mother and realize that its emotions are separate from other people.

From a cultural perspective, you can see this level of consciousness in stone-age people who thought themselves as a part of nature and tended to live by instinct and sensation. It is all about basic survival: food, shelter, reproduction, warmth. You can also see it in late-stage Alzheimer's patients, people living on the streets, people in starvation situations. Ken Wilber estimates that 1 percent of the world's population are in this category and they wield zero percent power in the world.

Magical Consciousness

Magical consciousness is generally displayed in children between the ages of two to seven. At this level, there is an inability to distinguish between the contents of the mind and those of the external world. It is an egocentric state where the whole world revolves around the child. You can see that in children's books. I once saw an illustration in one of Enid Blyton's books where the two main characters, Noddy and Big Ears, were coming home from an adventure in Noddy's car. They pass a signpost at the side of the road that just says "Home 4 miles." That assumes that the whole world revolves round these characters to the extent that road signs are all designed for them. They and the world are one and everything conspires to be a part of that one world inhabited by the child.

This level of consciousness sees the development of magical beliefs and invisible friends. The sun and moon follow us as we walk. Magic words exist, and by saying those words we cast spells or exert a power on our surroundings. We see fairy stories where the world conspires to help bring about the stories' resolution, like the briars growing in *Sleeping Beauty*. Witches cast spells, and spells can be broken by a kiss. Through interacting with others, the child gradually learns she or he is not the center of the world; one cannot magic things into place and one must cooperate and share.

From a cultural perspective, you can see this magical consciousness in tribal cultures not wanting you to take a picture of them, because that picture will give you power over them. Voodoo dolls are used, and natural phenomena can be controlled by "word" ceremonies such as rain dancing or some of the word ceremonies in religions, such as Holy Communion. This level of consciousness is strong in developing countries, in world religions, in gang culture, in athletic teams (superstitions), and even in corporate cultures where sales teams can also be highly superstitious. Wilber estimates that 10 percent of the world's population live in this level of consciousness, wielding 1 percent of the world's power.

Mythical Consciousness

This level of consciousness is essentially conformist and is exhibited by children of the age of seven and upward. Here there is an awareness of the concreteness of the world—parents, teachers, rocks, rules, laws. It is the "law-and-order" stage of development. What Daddy says is right or wrong *is* right or wrong: my parents right or wrong, my God right or wrong, my country right or wrong. At this level things are very black and white. Diversity causes confusion and the inner world of the child is populated by (powerful) Gods who have an effect; namely, parents and teachers. The child can get by if they are good, but will fall if they are bad; that is their experience. It no longer believes it can make the world do its bidding by magic, but by appealing to the "Gods"—whoever they may be.

Culturally this is the first emergence of the self as an individual different from the tribe. There is a strong belief in a moral "right way" and that this way has been handed down by others. This level of consciousness can be seen in nationalism, in concepts such as Crusades and Jihad. It is the dominant culture of world religions. Violating codes of behavior has severe repercussions. It is hierarchical, paternalistic, and people at this level are controlled by guilt and the pressure to conform. It is very evident in religion, Victorian England, codes of chivalry and patriotism. Wilber estimates that 60 percent of the world's population exist at this level, wielding 35 percent of the power.

Rational Consciousness

At this level children learn to rationalize and work things out for themselves. The death of mythical consciousness and the rebirth of rational consciousness begins in adolescence. It is characterized by the ability to think abstractly in accordance with the rules of logic. Culturally this is the dominant level of consciousness, and it is evident in universities, governments. The enlightenment lifted us culturally from the mythical level. Rational consciousness is achievement orientated and concerned with materialistic gain. It is evident in the market economy, militant atheism, the emerging middle classes, colonialism, the military, secular humanism, and liberal self-interest. Wilber estimates 30 percent of the world's population are in this area, wielding 50 percent of the world's power.

Visionary Consciousness

This level is individualistic and goes beyond simply thinking abstractly, but can think in three dimensions. There is an ability to make connections beyond current thinking. We begin to see the mind and the process of thinking as a part of the equation of working things out. There is a perception of the need to free the human spirit from greed. It involves egalitarianism, the value of communities, diversity, and multiculturalism.

Culturally, it involves the idea of "green thinking" and ecology. It is evident in postmodernism, humanistic psychology, Greenpeace, animal rights, political correctness, postcolonialism, human rights issues, diversity movements. Here Wilber says 10 percent of the population wield 15 percent of the power.

Soul Consciousness

Soul consciousness is a quantum shift in the goalposts. At this level, there is an awareness of ourselves as a part of something bigger than ourselves. We are a part of an order. The result at this level is an expanded vision. People are less attached to beliefs and there is a greater awareness of the role of the mind in shaping consciousness. Here there is the idea of all things being interconnected, a concept of a new spirituality as the meshwork of all existence.

Culturally you can see it in the mystics, in the work of Einstein, Gandhi, monasticism, compassionate living, acceptance, yoga, meditation, and the contemplative life. Wilber estimates 0.1 percent of the population are involved at this level with 1 percent of the power.

These levels of consciousness are only a rough guide, and you will find that they do not occur in our lives as a progression. Each of us will use different levels for different functions: When filling in our tax return, it is better to use rational consciousness. Using visionary consciousness to fill in the return may lead us to spending time at the invitation of our government.

Ask yourself which level of consciousness you use when dealing with your children, and which your health. Which in business and which in sport? Which in religion, in politics, in leisure, with the environment, with war? We pick and choose as and when we like. And so, our being is subject to different influences depending on what we are doing and where we focus and that may seem pretty basic; however, most of the time we go about our lives as if these levels do not exist.

We might profess to be spiritual and sign up to the interconnectedness of all things. But when it comes to the way we look after our money, or our house, or our family, or our health, we often assume that there will be no intelligent design unless we put it there ourselves. We fundamentally do not trust that life will turn out the way we want it to. And so, we have to do this work for ourselves. That is how most of us run our lives.

True, we might consider letting go on our yoga mat or on our meditation cushion, but the moment we get up from there we are alert once more to how we need to shape our lives to have them go our way. But what if the very act of trying to control our lives was the very thing that was getting in the way? That the order that we try to impose on our lives is like weighting a car wheel so that it could not possibly go straight. What if life naturally worked out—and the thing that screwed it up was our attempt to make it go our own way?

Chapter 2
Stuff Happens

So far we have looked at the difference between the order we see in the world and the disorder we experience in our lives and how religions try to explain that disorder through their beliefs.

We have looked at the possibility of an order that lies within us that may or may not be linked to some sort of caring Life-Force that takes the order of the world and makes sense of the order in our lives.

Our expression in our lives is a function of our being. And our being comes from the way we look at the world.

But life still rarely goes the way we want it to. We might have a pretty straight run for a while, and then someone dies, or our partner leaves us, or our job goes pear-shaped. You fill in the blanks. And when that does happen we feel out of control all over again. When British prime minister Harold MacMillan was asked what he most feared, he said, "Events, dear boy, events." They come upon us all and simply prove that we haven't a clue as to what is going on.

The point is that in reality, although the universe is ordered, most of us experience our lives as chaotic. We might give the appearance of being in control, but deep down everyone is just scrambling to stay afloat. Even politicians who always seem so unflappable are generally making it up as they go along, or at least their aides are. People in authority give off that look of being all knowing, but they are really just the same as all of us: They eat, they go to the restroom, and when something really challenging happens they have the same response that we all have: "Oh shit!"

Creating Our Own Order

Order seems hard to come by. And yet anyone who has ever been involved in meditation, yoga, or mindfulness knows that the key to that internal order is a still mind. Just as events and circumstances seem to swirl around us and we seem to be at the effect of the "slings and arrows of outrageous fortune,"[1] so our minds similarly often exist in a state of chaos. We flit from one worry to the next and generally stir up our emotions to such a state that we are unable to contain them. The key to that interior stillness, that interior order, is to still the mind and rest in the silence of the interior gaze.

Meister Eckhart, a fourteenth-century German mystic, said that the perfect interior stance, the perfect meditative stance was to be of the attitude where you realize that, in the particular moment, you actually want for nothing. There is nothing that you need. You have everything necessary for sitting in that interior stance. And because you need nothing, there is nothing for you to do. Nothing for you to make happen, nothing for you to will; and in that place of wanting for nothing and willing nothing, it is necessary to acknowledge that you know nothing. That all your marvelous ideas add up to a hill of beans when it comes to working out the grand scheme of things. They are all guesses and borrowed wisdom. We have no idea how it all works, and what our place is within it, so we might as well admit it, and own up to knowing nothing, which means we are not trying to predict what will happen next, or what should happen, or even what conceivably might happen. We therefore give up all pretense of knowing and enter into the place of not knowing, a far richer and broader place than our poor attempts at "getting it right."

So Meister Eckhart suggests that the true meditative stance, the true interior stance is one of "Wanting for Nothing, Willing Nothing, and Knowing Nothing." He describes this as true poverty. Not engaging with the richness of our ideas, or the marvelousness of our thoughts, but instead being in a place where we are satisfied with our experience, we are not trying to change it, or make it different, and we are choosing to realize that we do not know anything either. This is a totally open stance. We are open to our thoughts, but not engaging them, we are open to our feelings, but not indulging in them, we are open to what our body feels like, but not trying to change it, and we are not claiming to know anything of what it all means.

Being in this place opens us up to the present moment. The interior stance is simply the stance of being present to everything that is going on without trying to change it, and it is through this interior stance that we begin to touch the nature of interior order. By just being present we are able to realize the order that is at the center of all things. Eliot's "Still point in a turning world." It is at this point that we experience the order. We are therefore the ones who can give order to the chaos around us, to not be at the effect of whatever comes our way, but to realize that we have the order we seek within us, and through connecting with that order we are able to bring some of it into our lives. That is why meditation and yoga are often called a spiritual "practice," because we are practicing being in a place of order, by creating that order in an interior stance, and by quietening our mind. We begin to have the possibility of bringing order to our exterior world.

What are the chances that our interior world is connected to the exterior world? Obviously, if our mind is less chaotic, so our behavior will be less chaotic, and therefore our exterior lives will be less chaotic. But what if it were more than that? Like the idea in quantum physics of the observer having an effect on the experiment. What if our interior stance actually had an effect on what was going on around us? That being the "still point in the turning world" somehow made the world turn less, or in a different way? Our inner world having an effect on our outer world.

Non-Duality

We are forever suffering because of the difference between the inner world and the outer world. Our expectation of the outer world is not being met. We are unable to control either world; we often cannot control how we think and feel, and we equally cannot control what goes on out there. So how do we reconcile the two?

Well, the first thing to consider is the possibility that there are not two worlds, but our inner world and our outer world are both manifestations of the same reality. The whole idea of non-duality is bound up with this.

Non-duality means "not two" or "one undivided without a second." As the dictionary says: Non-dualism primarily refers to a mature state of consciousness, in which the dichotomy of I-other is "transcended," and awareness is described as "centerless" and "without dichotomies." In other words, the whole idea that all reality is one and that we, in here, are separate from everything "out there," is an illusion.

We think we are separate by virtue of the fact that we feel separate. I can feel my hands and my body, I can see you as separate "out there," but in reality this idea suggests that there is one unitive consciousness, one form of life, one being that is expressed in many forms, with many heads and many bodies; that although we feel that there is me, and the rest of you out there, in reality we are all of a one, and that includes what we think of as our inner reality and what we think of as our outer reality. They are both fundamentally connected, and to see one as separate from the other is, in fact, an illusion.

This may be all fine and dandy as an idea; however, it does not always square with the fact that our experience tells us something different. It tells us that we are separate, and that our inner reality is often very different from the outer reality.

When you think of life as those two realities—the inner and the outer—it all becomes about having one reality conform to the other. Either we try to make the outer reality come under the control of the inner reality, which Howard Hughes found out was impossible, no matter how much money and power you have, or your inner reality has to conform to the outer reality, in which case you end up denying that inner reality and just giving up. In both cases there is a battle that is going on and a struggle, which does not necessarily lead to peace.

When you consider the idea that there is one reality, then it is possible to live life from a very different perspective. You can see the inner world and the outer world as being reflections of each other, and as such both are operating together. That perspective suggests that if we do not try to change the outer reality, when it does not match up to our inner expectations, we let go of our expectations, and we let go of wanting to try to make our outer worlds conform to our inner ideas. That does not mean to say that we give up trying to have an effect on life. We do not simply align ourselves to one side or the other. No, instead we use different tools to navigate ourselves around our lives.

Inner World vs. Outer World

Quantum mechanics tells us that the inner world of the observer has an effect on the outer world of the experiment. It says that all of reality is relational. And that gives credence to our idea of there being one reality rather than two. So if we are living in one reality, and our inner world and our outer world are in fact a part of the same reality, how does that affect the way that we deal with the process of living?

Well, first of all it forces us to be much more discerning. We have to look at what is going on around us and be aware of the impact we are having. In the Tao Te Ching, Lao Tzu says that the master *"thinks of his enemy as the shadow that he himself casts."*[2] And that makes a difference to the way that we deal with our enemy. It is not to say that we do not deal with things in our outer reality that need to be dealt with, just that we look to the effect that we ourselves might be having on the situation.

In life we are asked to always respond in the most loving way, and that includes bringing compassion and understanding to bear when we might be out of control. If we are in a concentration camp, we cannot magic ourselves out of that situation. Nor have we to say that it is all my fault that I am here. Rather we have to look and see what we are able to bring to that situation, from our inner reserves, and from our understanding of what is going on around us. Similarly, if we are in a situation of grief or despair of one sort or another, we cannot expect that to be changed by simply changing our outer reality; if only I had enough money I would be OK, if only I had my health, if only I had a partner. We have to realize that simply by changing the outer reality we will not necessarily feel any better.

It is like an egg. Our outer world is the shell, our inner world the yoke. And yet it is a whole in itself. The inner world, the yoke, cannot take a bit of the outer world, the shell, to make itself better; it has to have its own balance, just as the outer world has its balance, and the two together make the whole. So, our inner life has to be whole in itself, not demanding that the outer world change to make it better. We have to be able to be at peace with ourselves internally. To be OK with ourselves whatever the circumstances. To not look for something in the outer world to complete us, because we are complete.

There is a famous stanza from the Dhammapada, the sayings of the Buddha:

> It is not good conduct that helps you on the way.
> Nor ritual,
> Nor book learning,
> Nor withdrawal into the self.
> Nor deep meditation.
> None of these confer mastery and joy.
> O Seeker!
> Rely on nothing
> Until you want nothing![3]

In other words, to rely on something outside ourselves to make us feel complete is not helpful. The only really helpful attitude is to realize that we are already complete. We do not need ideas about what will make us whole, and we do not need to try to get things

21

or do things to make us whole. We are already whole, and we need nothing to complete us.

Both worlds have an integrity in themselves, and to try to make one world magically make the other one better simply does not work, because integrity is at the heart of the relationship between the two perceived realities, and allows us to experience them as one reality. Integrity itself means wholeness, "soundness, wholeness, completeness," figuratively from integer meaning "whole." Integrity between what we perceive as our inner world and our outer world brings about the wholeness that we seek as we battle between the two.

If you look up the idea of the inner world and the outer world, most people will want to say that the outer world is a reflection of the inner world, that if you are internally hateful, you will see the outer world as hateful, and if you are inwardly loving you will see the outer world as loving; and there is some truth in that, but I think it goes further, in that what we are looking at is not just the reflection, but also the two worlds being congruent with each other. Congruent from *congruere*, literally "to come together, agree, correspond with."

When the two worlds we experience are congruent with each other, when they agree with each other, when they come together, then we have an integrity that produces a whole. You cannot possibly be mean and miserly and expect to experience the world as being generous to you. Your inner experience has to be congruent with what is going on around you.

There is a lot going on in the world, and just to be nice is not enough, which is why it takes discernment. We are all a part of creation, and evolution. We are all evolving all the time, and to be aware of that evolution enables us to roll with it, and in being a part of creation and evolution, we are subject to the unfolding of the universe and that includes those two perceived realities, the inner and the outer.

We have to be aware of the outer unfolding and the inner unfolding as everything is part of the same evolution. Both are evolving at the same time, as one affects the other. The material world is evolving, and so is our consciousness. So the inner promptings that we have must be listened to, but only insofar as they are congruent with what is going on outside. There is no point in grieving over loss of your health when in fact what you have to deal with is the very act of getting better. There is no point in continually revisiting the past, when in fact you are now being asked to deal with the present. The two realities have a natural congruence, and to live life skillfully is to discern what the congruence is. When we do that the two realities become one and we have integrity.

Little things like giving up alcohol for a short period of time gives us integrity, because we experience a decision made in our inner reality being made real in our outer reality; and if we are an alcoholic, then permanently giving up alcohol is a way of us having that integrity and wholeness by putting ourselves in a place that is appropriate to our situation. We acknowledge, for example, that for the inner world and the outer world to be congruent, we have to give up alcohol. In that sense, our actions are the bridge between our inner world and our outer world, and our actions enable us to make the two worlds congruent and give us the integrity to experience the one reality—the whole.

So, in effect we are participating in a dance, our inner sensibilities, our outer sensitivity, and action that brings the two together. We hold our partner of the outer world, listen to the music, and together we dance the dance of life, and become the whole that we aspire to. Of course the other bridge is our breath, which is why we often concentrate on breath in meditation or yoga. Bringing the outer world into us, holding it, and letting it go. Through the breath we experience the unified whole. And by experiencing that unified whole, we can sometimes then trip into that experience of unitive consciousness. The actual experiences of the inner and the outer worlds are a unified whole. Through our breath we are able to experience the wholeness of life, and when we let go of the attachment to our minds—the source of the illusion of separation—the illusion disappears and we are left with the reality of wholeness—unitive consciousness, satori, or enlightenment.

That is why practices such as meditation and yoga are key in reconciling that experience of separation with the actuality of wholeness. We cannot do it on our own, we cannot think our way into that place, and so we have to work on it. We must work on giving up the ideas we have about separation, and use our breath to realize the unified nature of consciousness; that involves forgiveness, grace, sensitivity, love, compassion, stillness, awareness, inclusivity, all the tools that are at our disposal to become actualized as a part of the whole that is moving and evolving into that fullness.

Through this we are being asked to bring order to the stuff that happens, to the events. The place of order is within us, and by bringing our hearts to bear on situations we transform them. We do that through practice, literally taking that time every day to practice bringing order from our hearts to our minds, and therefore eventually bringing that order into the world. But we are still faced with the issue of knowing when to act and when not to act, how to actually live the Life-Force within us.

Not Being in Control

No matter how hard we try to be spiritual, we still have our two natures competing with each other. The inner and the outer. And somehow, we have to decide when to act and when not to act. It happens on a big level. Do I go to college or not? Do I take this job or not? Do I go out with this person? Do I move to a new house? It also happens on a small level. Do I stay an extra ten minutes at the party, or do I go for a hike now? Shall I have that extra hot dog? Shall I go to that film?

It is a sobering thought that every decision you make bears on every other decision. Just waiting five minutes at the party can mean that you get in your car five minutes late and as you turn out of the drive you do not get hit and killed, but instead miss your fate, not even knowing that it might have been a possibility. "Sliding Doors" territory. One decision sets up the next decision, which in turn makes up your hour, then your day, then your life.

We are always thinking about it: How can we make any decision with confidence? To think about it too much is to go mad; and the events and circumstances just keep on coming. Sometimes the pace seems almost too much to bear. And at those times we just have to remember that it is not about us.

The Franciscan friar and author Richard Rohr says that there are five things that a man needs to learn in order to pass through adolescence into manhood:

1. Life is hard.
2. You are not that important.
3. Your life is not about you.
4. You are not in control.
5. You are going to die.

Those are the things that keep us humble and enable us to remember that we are not in control; and that is such an important thing to remember. No matter how much we try to be in control, the sane thing, from the Latin word *Sanus*, meaning healthy, is to realize that we are not in control of our life, or our circumstances.

In this book we have set up this question of our relationship with the Life-Force. No matter how we try to force life in one direction or another, we are not in control. People who think they are in control end up going mad. That Life-Force is going to take you down whatever way you turn: It is going to end badly for all of us; and every moment of the day, that Life-Force is having its way with us. There is not a second that we are in control, at least of circumstances.

So, what are we in control of? Our bodies? Well, no, they rebel all the time. Illness, pain, weakness, puberty, menopause—we just live in our bodies hoping they are going to get us through. Our minds— yes, surely our minds. By being spiritually minded and practicing mindfulness surely we can be in control? As Holocaust survivor and psychiatrist Victor Frankl said, *"Between stimulus and response, there is a space. In that space is our power to choose our response. In our response lies our growth and our freedom."*

There is our control. And yet even that is only temporary. More often than not we lose it when things go awry. So, most of the time we are not actually in control, even when we think we are. That is not to say that we should not try to make things work the way we want them to. It is good to put food on the table and a roof over our heads and to put the children through school. It's just that we should not kid ourselves that, ultimately, we are in control. Even those who can make everything in the world go right still get brought up short. Look at Steve Jobs.

So, it is an important step of sanity to realize that we are not in control. And in doing that we begin to see our lives in their proper perspective. We begin to get that paradox of being in control while realizing that we are not in control; and that is the paradox of the question around living with that Life-Force.

Of course, we have to get our stuff together. To turn up on time, to get dressed, to cook our meals, to pay the rent. But, in reality, we are out of control. So how do we deal with our being out of control? How do we square that with the process of living?

Well, obviously it is in this place that we begin to look at how to cooperate with that Life-Force that seems to throw us about so outrageously.

We have to develop a sensitivity that is not looking to get into control, but one that enables us to be in balance while out of control. Like turning into the skid with the car, or leaning into the turn with skis; we have to go with whatever is happening and realize that there is something deeper that we have to relate to. I think that this Life-Force comes to us in the circumstances of our lives, and asks us to relate to that presence rather than the circumstances. There is an inner balance that we have to reach for that will contain the circumstances. That still point in a turning world. We have to become that still point.

In a storm, on a gyroscope, in a centrifuge, the only point that is not moving is the eye of the storm, the balance point of the gyroscope, the central point of the centrifuge. Be anywhere else and you are thrown about. We have to become the eye of the storm that is our lives; and to do that we have to let go. To let go of our desire to control the outcomes, and focus on just being in what is going on.

As it says in the Tao Te Ching:

> Do your work, then step back.
> The only path to serenity.[4]

Our "out of controlness" is really a function of us being attached to the outcomes in our life. But we do not know what is going to happen from one moment to the next, nor what that moment means for our future.

There is a lovely story about a Chinese farmer who had only one horse. One morning he woke to find the horse gone. All his friends came around to commiserate. "What bad luck," they said, "your only horse." The farmer looked at them impassively and said, "Good luck? Bad luck? Who knows?" The next week the farmer woke to find his paddock full of horses. His one horse had returned and brought with him a herd of wild horses from the hills. The farmer's friends returned, and this time wanted to celebrate. "What good luck," they said. The farmer again looked at them impassively and said, "Good luck? Bad luck? Who knows?" The next day the farmer's only son began to break in the new horses, and while working on the very first one he was thrown to the ground and broke his leg badly. "What bad luck," his friends said. But the farmer again replied, "Good luck? Bad luck? Who knows?" Later in the month the Emperor declared war, and the army came to take away all the men from the village, all except the farmer's son because he had a broken leg. Good luck, bad luck, who knows?

Good Luck, Bad Luck, Who Knows?

We think we know when something is good or bad, and we try to steer our lives toward what we think is good ... but the truth is, we really don't know. We don't know what is good and bad in life.

Even Adam and Eve were taught this: "*but you must not eat from the tree of the knowledge of good and evil.*"[5] By letting go of our attachment to the outcomes in our life, we suddenly become centered on what is actually going on, and that is what is important. Suddenly we do not have our eyes fixed on the so-called prize; suddenly we have our eyes fixed on what we are doing, for the sake of doing it; and at that moment we become in touch with who we really are, doing what we are really doing, in the moment that we are doing it. Suddenly you are in a new place. You are beginning to be in that moment with the Life-Force, rather than trying to force life. You are still conscious of what is going on. You are still paying the rent and putting dinner on the table, but a part of you realizes that no matter what you are doing, there are other forces at play—literally the weather of our life—and we stay at the center of that weather. We stay at the point where we remain in touch with our Life-Force, letting go of our preoccupation with circumstances. We notice our fears, and we just let them go and come back into the present. It is something to take into a practice, into a daily meditation or yoga practice.

In his book *The Perennial Philosophy*, Aldous Huxley defines Leibniz's phrase 'Philosophia perennis' as "The psychology that finds in the soul something similar to, or even identical with, Divine Reality."[6]

When we find that place at the eye of the storm, then we have found the still point in the turning world. We are in contact with the point where intelligent design is taking place, both within us and outside us. As Huxley says, the Perennial Philosophy is also "the metaphysic that recognizes a Divine Reality substantial to the word of things and lives and minds."[7] So, it is not only within us, it is also at the same time "out there." It is both in the eye of the storm, and in the storm itself. We achieve that balance when we are unattached to the outcomes of our life.

Actively Passive or Passively Active?

It is difficult to be unattached. How can we be when we so desperately care about what goes on in our life? We care what happens to our health, our wealth, our children. Yet, in spite of the amount we are invested in all that, we have to realize that the creation of the course of our lives does not come about by our controlling the circumstances. It comes by our managing the way we relate to those self-same circumstances.

Whatever happens to us, it is within our power to contain it; and it is within our power to rest in the idea that there is an order deeper than those circumstances. Whether we have judged those circumstances to be good or bad, we have the power to contain them within our hearts. If we have the presence of mind to do so, we can draw on something that is deeper than the outward goings-on—something that connects with the order that is at the heart of the universe, something that exists within us. And it is here that we find Einstein's idea of a friendly universe.

Something deeper is offering us a challenge: to deal with the experience of what is going on, however painful, at that deep level, and thereby effect a real transformation in our lives. Or to simply react to the circumstances and operate out of our pain, anger, or fear of what is going on. In other words, by bringing something of our essence into the situation, and focusing on that rather than the circumstances themselves, we can bring about an order and depth that belies the chaos that we are normally subjected to. And I am suggesting that the action that we use to bring this about is to live in an "actively passive" stance.

Lao Tzu says in the Tao Te Ching:

> The ancient Masters were profound and subtle.
> Their wisdom was unfathomable.
> There is no way to describe it;
> all we can describe is their appearance.
>
> They were careful
> as someone crossing an iced-over stream.
> Alert as a warrior in enemy territory.
> Courteous as a guest.
> Fluid as melting ice.
> Shapable as a block of wood.
> Receptive as a valley.
> Clear as a glass of water.
>
> Do you have the patience to wait
> till your mud settles and the water is clear?
> Can you remain unmoving
> till the right action arises by itself?
>
> The Master doesn't seek fulfillment.
> Not seeking, not expecting,
> she is present, and can welcome all things.[8]

That sums up the stance of being actively passive: not seeking, not expecting, but being present so we can welcome all things.

Khalil Gibran says in his stanza on pain:

> And could you keep your heart in wonder at the
> daily miracles of your life, your pain would not seem
> less wondrous than your joy;
> And you would accept the seasons of your heart,
> even as you have always accepted the seasons that
> pass over your fields.
> And you would watch with serenity through the
> winters of your grief.

So, our first step is letting go of these outcomes: Not to stop striving for things, but not to be so invested in whether or not they happen. As Lao Tzu says,

> Do your work, then step back.
> The only path to serenity.

And then there is the second step.

> Do you have the patience to wait
> till your mud settles and the water is clear?
> Can you remain unmoving
> till the right action arises by itself?

That is just as difficult. We always want to rush in and fix things the moment they seem out of kilter. But the actively passive stance is one of wakeful conscious readiness that does not rush in, but waits until right action arises by itself.

Victor Frankl again: "Between stimulus and response, there is a space. In that space is our power to choose our response. In our response lies our growth and our freedom."

But this stance is more than just waiting to respond, pausing before rushing in. It comes from a deeper place that says, as in the words of Julian of Norwich, "All will be well, and all manner of things will be well."

It comes from a deep conviction that fundamentally life is turning in the right direction, and that if we let it turn in our lives, then something new, something beyond our expectation, a horizon that we had not previously seen will appear. This is so different from the "passively active" stance, where we just carry on with activity because it just seems the only option. That way of living values the activity itself—doing something for the sake of doing something.

29

And most of us are prone to that. We hate to be "inactive"; it is seen as weak, weak in our personal lives, and weak in political life.

We think we are doing something, when in fact we are just going through the motions. Tit-for-tat diplomatic expulsions after an incident, reading the riot act to a family member, there are any number of automatic responses that we are prone to putting into practice rather than just waiting till the mud clears and right action arises by itself.

We are limited by our imagination, what we think we could do, what might happen in our lives. Our horizons are limited by what we can imagine. Think of the best that could happen in your life. If all the chips fell your way, how would it turn out for you? Having thought of that, I want you to consider that life might be able to deliver to you something that is beyond your wildest dreams. It could offer you horizons that you could never have imagined; and it follows that you are therefore being limited by your imagination by being limited to what you think is possible.

If you had told me forty years ago that I would be working as an ordained minister in Aspen, Colorado, I would not have believed you. Forty years ago, the extent of my horizon involved yachts, girls, and private islands. I thought that was it; and yet the wealth I experience now is infinitely greater than those yachts and islands and girls. After all, wealth is the ability to appreciate experience. It is not money in the bank or net value. You can have all that and still be miserable. No, it is the ability to appreciate experience, the extent to which you can experience and appreciate what you are experiencing. Without that appreciation, there is no value. You need the appreciation to create the value.

In fact, the word appreciation comes from the Latin word *appretiatus*, which means "to set a price to." In other words, the creation of value is in our own hands. And when that is expanded, when your very horizons of wealth are expanded, so the possibilities for your life are expanded.

In other words, I am saying that this stance of being actively passive actually enables us to appreciate value. It is saying, "I will wait till the right action arises by itself, waiting for something greater than I could have ever imagined happening. Something from the Life-Force which is driving my life. I am going to let that have free reign and see what it brings."

Funnily enough that is the very aim of the Lord's prayer.

The purpose of those words is to put us in a stance so that whatever is happening you can hold it within the words and see the wisdom that comes to you through having to relate to the circumstances.

Father of us,
The One who is in the heavens;
Hallowed be your nature
May your kingdom come,
May your will be done,
as in heaven, so on earth.
Give us today our bread from above
that gives our whole life meaning.
Cancel our debts,
As we cancel the accounts of those
indebted towards us.
And let us not be led into temptation,
but deliver us from evil.

I was given this translation by John Pettival, a Bible scholar, and it is the one I have used ever since.

The purpose of this set of words is to take us into the perfect attitude to relate to our lives from that deeper perspective. Each phrase deals with a different aspect of the way we look at our lives, and shapes us so that we can see the challenge in the circumstances that we face.

Father of us,

Acknowledges that the universe is a friendly place, that there is an "other" to relate to, and that other has a loving disposition toward us.

The One who is in the heavens;

Places that "other" in relationship to our lives. It is within us, it is all around us. We are like a living sponge at the bottom of the seabed with the ocean in and around the creature.

Hallowed be your nature

Puts us in the correct relationship to that deeper order. Literally "may your being be regarded by me with a sense of respect and reverence." We acknowledge that all we can do in the presence of this intelligent design is to bow down and give up to its magnificence.

May your kingdom come,

May your loving nature come to order all things. We give up to the wisdom and love that is present in the essence of that being, and allow it to order us and all that is around us.

May your will be done, as in heaven, so on earth

Come and inhabit my life. May my life conform to your purposes as I acknowledge that this game is yours, and I am a part of that game. Wherever you are, you bring about perfection, so bring perfection into my life.

Give us today our bread from above that gives our whole life meaning.

Give meaning to my life—may I see my place in this bigger picture and in so doing know what to do in any given situation.

Cancel our debts,
As we cancel the accounts of those indebted towards us.

May I let go of any attachments I have in this life, and so be able to focus on that deeper level. And in so doing may I let go of anything that I am holding on to with regard to other people.

And let us not be led into temptation, but deliver us from evil.

And may I not be put in situations where I feel the need to choose between your way and my own way so that I may not take to myself things that are not naturally given to me.

And then from the traditional form:

For the kingdom, the power and the glory are yours.

For everything I participate with in this life comes from you. All power comes from you, and all thanks, for anything I receive in this life, goes to you.

Now and forever

In this present moment, which lasts for eternity.

Amen

So be it.

I have been using this set of words almost every day for the last thirty years and they always work. They put you in exactly the right place to deal with whatever comes your way in life. It takes you right through all the various stages that lead to an attitude of acceptance of what is so: namely, the existence of a guiding Life-Force; that this is within us; that it is sacred; that we want it to consume us so that we will conform to its will; that we understand our place and its purpose for us; that we will leave behind all other attachments, and give ourselves fully into it; now and forever. It is a mind-blowing journey of only a few short sentences, and it can transform your life. It can also bring answers to problems. Sometimes I have been faced with something that I cannot work out, and I use this set of words and a solution miraculously appears. It seems to draw from somewhere very deep and shortcut our access to that divine consciousness.

There is also that famous verse in the Bible: *"What good will it be for someone to gain the whole world, yet forfeit their soul?"*[9]

And all of this speaks to the nature of humility.

The twentieth-century monk Thomas Merton says: "You do not need to know precisely what is happening, or where it is all going. What you need is to recognize the possibilities and challenges offered by the present moment and embrace them with courage, faith and hope."

If we could but see the gift that we have in our lives, then gratitude and humility is surely the only response; and yet we take it all for granted. More than that, we demand more, we complain, we argue, we beseech, we long for greener grass, we fight, we take, we demand. We forget the gift that is in front of us.

Humility is our true response to life. It puts us in exactly the right place with regards to everything that happens. We naturally become the guest house that Rumi spoke of in his poem "The Guest House":

> This being human is a guest house.
> Every morning a new arrival.
>
> A joy, a depression, a meanness,
> some momentary awareness comes
> as an unexpected visitor.
>
> Welcome and entertain them all!
> Even if they are a crowd of sorrows,
> who violently sweep your house
> empty of its furniture,
> still, treat each guest honorably.
> He may be clearing you out
> for some new delight.
>
> The dark thought, the shame, the malice
> meet them at the door laughing and invite them in.
>
> Be grateful for whatever comes.
> because each has been sent
> as a guide from beyond.[10]

And in that state of humility we do welcome them all, because we recognize our own poverty. Everything is a gift, because we came into this world with nothing. Having arrived at that point we are in a place of true humility and so able to see the wealth of what is before us. When we know we have nothing, and then look around and see all that there is to appreciate, then we can become truly wealthy.

As Jesus said: "Consider how the lilies grow: They do not labor or spin. Yet I tell you, not even Solomon in all his glory was adorned like one of these. If that is how God clothes the grass of the field, which is here today and tomorrow is thrown into the furnace, how much more will He clothe you."[11]

A position of the knowledge of wealth comes from humility, which is exactly the opposite of how the world looks at it. In reality, the position of humility is the only way to achieve real wealth. To really see the trees, to appreciate being in community, to see the beauty in everyone's faces, the light as it comes through the windows, the sound of silence. You have to recognize your emptiness, in order to be filled with such wealth.

Again:

> It is not good conduct that helps you on the way.
> Nor ritual,
> Nor book learning,
> Nor withdrawal into the self.
> Nor deep meditation.
> None of these confer mastery and joy.
> O Seeker!
> Rely on nothing
> Until you want nothing!

That is the actively passive stance. Look at Jesus in the last days of his life. Up to Judas's kiss he was all action, healing, upbraiding, and leading his disciples. After that kiss, he became actively passive. Allowing himself to be taken, because he knew that he was not in the hands of his captors, but the hands of something greater. It is such a powerful set of images—Pilate, the scourging, right through to the Crucifixion. An actively passive stance. But where will that leave us? Being actively passive may not at first sight seem a place that we would want to go.

Chapter 3
The Big "Out There"

Being actively passive does not seem a likely place to get results. The smart money in life is to make it all happen, to be a success, to get to Harvard, become a politician, or a captain of industry, or a lawyer, or raise a family. Drive our lives through to the point where we can look back and see what we have made of ourselves; and you see it in the driven lives people lead.

Mick Jagger, Pablo Picasso, Barak Obama, Richard Branson, Albert Einstein, Thomas Edison, Babe Ruth, Tom Brokaw, Usain Bolt, Harrison Ford, Oprah Winfrey: These are all people with great careers who have made something of their lives. Consider the will, the determination that they must have exerted to succeed in the way that they have done. And in doing so, many of them have benefited others with their achievements. The *New York Times* obits are full of such people and what they have made of their lives, and they are all an inspiration to the next generation of people who follow them and try to emulate their success.

So how do you square all of this with the idea of being actively passive? Not being concerned with the outcome of circumstances? Well, I think the first thing to say is that there is nothing wrong with success and achievement. It is just that we should not be attached to it as an outcome.

Lao Tzu says in the Tao Te Ching:

> The ancient Masters were profound and subtle.
> Their wisdom was unfathomable.
> There is no way to describe it;
> all we can describe is their appearance.
>
> They were careful
> as someone crossing an iced-over stream.
> Alert as a warrior in enemy territory.
> Courteous as a guest.
> Fluid as melting ice.

Shapable as a block of wood.
Receptive as a valley.
Clear as a glass of water.

Do you have the patience to wait
till your mud settles and the water is clear?
Can you remain unmoving
till the right action arises by itself?

The Master doesn't seek fulfillment.
Not seeking, not expecting,
she is present, and can welcome all things.[8]

It is the attachment to the outcome that leads to the problem, the fact that we do not do our work and step back. We do our work, and if it does not have the desired effect, we tinker around with it. We are more invested in a particular outcome than we are in the work for its own sake. We want the promotion, we want the book to be a success, we want the person we are interested in to be interested in us. It is the outcome we want, not the work.

But you have to remember those five points of maturity that Richard Rohr came up with:

1. Life is hard.
2. You are not that important.
3. Your life is not about you.
4. You are not in control.
5. You are going to die.

At first sight, they do not seem very inspiring; in fact, they can seem a complete downer. Life being hard, us not being important, our life not being about us, our not being in control, and on top of that we are all going to die. Give me another drink, barman. But in reality, these principles are actually sobering thoughts. Thoughts that bring us to a point of sanity—health. In life, we are all looking for basic laws that we can depend on, and these principles provide that. And in the area of being actively passive, the key point is that your life is not about you.

So many of us in the development of our great career think that our lives are about us. Well, obviously from the way we see it they are. But if you are able to take that expanded vision, then they are not. There is an old joke about the woman who is playing the nurse in a production of *Romeo and Juliet*, and someone asks her what the play is about. She answers, "Well, there is this nurse, you see ...".

While we look at our lives from that perspective we will always be looking at our own careers before anything else. You really get it when you see a bouquet of flowers, it is not about any one flower. It is about the whole. When you look at the earth from space, it is not about any one country, it is about the earth.

The same is true about our lives, they are not about us. We are here for a purpose, but that purpose is not about us. We are here for the good of the whole, and unless we can get that, we cannot make the contribution we were put here to make.

Each of us is here because of a 1 in 20 million chance. Twenty million sperm are released to race toward the egg, and you won. Each of us won a race against 20 million others, and it is worth acknowledging the fact that you most definitely beat the odds. You came through. Why? Because you wanted it more than the others. You wanted to express yourself in your own unique way. But if we forget that we are also here because we are an expression of that Life-Force that we have been talking about, then we miss the point. Yes, we made it there first, but there was something in that Life-Force that impelled us in the first place. We are a manifestation of that Life-Force and its desire to express itself. And it has always been thus. As such, we are a part of something bigger than ourselves, both in terms of that Life-Force, and in terms of our world.

We are coming into an era of global consciousness. In the modern era, it began with television—the "global village" where we began to see into each other's backyards. Economics followed with the rise of the corporation and the worldwide movement of jobs and raw materials, and then the Internet set the seal on the deal, and made sure there was no going back by enabling mass communication at a micro and a macro level. And it is not just about economics. It is a reflection of a shift in the way we perceive the world.

The Gaia theory was an idea put forward by James Lovelock, arguing that living matter on the earth collectively defines and regulates the material conditions necessary for the continuance of life. The planet, or rather the biosphere, is thus likened to a vast self-regulating organism. If the planet is one great biosphere, that makes all of us human beings the flower of our planet, the most beautiful and precious part of that biosphere.

The only problem is that, like the giant hogweed, we are taking over the planet to the detriment of that biosphere. At some point in the world's history we, as a species, will have to learn that fact, or we will not survive. The planet will always survive, it has the time, the millions of years it needs to heal itself. We do not have that long.

We are the flower of the planet, and we are all moving toward planetary consciousness. I do not normally like to repeat unverified information, but sometimes stories are so good they should be true. Apparently, the thing that changes a "Neanderthal person" into a fully self-reflecting "human being" is the appearance of the 7 billionth neuron in the brain. When there are those 7 billion neurons in place, the brain develops the ability to think in a different way, and hence we have a human. We now have 7 billion people living on the planet, and if each person represented a neuron, and the planet is seen as an organism in itself, then the way the planet thinks about itself is changing. And that results in development of this "global consciousness": the planet reflecting on itself in a new way.

How Did It All Start?

Well, to answer that question we have to go right back to the big bang. At the big bang, particles were thrown out—the essence of those particles is the atoms that we know today; particles with a nucleus, protons, and electrons flying around them. This is what keeps them stable. But they also react to whatever is around them, and in that sense, they have a kind of reactive consciousness, just as a plant does.

So, matter comes flying out. That matter forms planets that heat and cool, one of the planets is the earth, those same atoms make life; and we human beings, made of those same atoms, become conscious and self-aware. We are aware of ourselves as being a part of the universe. In fact, we are all 13.7 billion years old, at least our atoms are. We are all a part of evolution, and the evolution I am talking about is not the one that grows an extra thumb for texting. I am talking about the evolution of consciousness.

However you look at it, everything started with the big bang 13.7 billion years ago. That was the beginning of the cosmos. So here we are, as humans, a part of the universe, a part of the big bang, but now conscious.

You are the universe made conscious of itself.

That ordering that began with the big bang has ended up with us all looking out into the world and saying, wow, look at that! There was a latent consciousness in those original carbon atoms that developed and evolved, and as it did so it brought itself together to make more and more complicated forms of that consciousness, and we are the end product of that. We are the flower of all of that.

So global consciousness is really the next step on that road. It seems to me that it would be such a shame to have to wait for an alien invasion or some huge global disaster to happen before we all come together and realize that we are a community, and that we have to solve one another's problems as well as our own. Otherwise, those problems will revisit us in other ways. Poverty and pollution in China is just as much a problem for the United States as unemployment and wage disparity in the United States is a problem for China; and for us to come to terms with this there has to be a shift in the way we all see the world, a shift in consciousness.

What we are seeing now is a part of that. People all over the planet are wanting something more. The universe has been around for 13.7 billion years. Humanity for considerably less. This change in consciousness will take time and will not necessarily be either pretty or smooth. There is no "smooth transition of power" when it comes to evolution. But it is coming, and it is progress, whether we like it or not.

Einstein said that "no problem can be solved from the same level of consciousness that created it," and for us to move through this with everyone on board, we need to look at it from a new level of consciousness; and this shift in global consciousness will give us a way to deal with the world's problems—if we are conscious enough at the level of our leadership to allow this to happen.

There is a lovely story about a guru who was asked by a pupil: "Master, how do we look after others?" The guru thought for a while and then answered the pupil: "There are no others." That is the change of consciousness that is arising. The idea that it is all about "we" rather than "they," "us" rather than "them."

In the book *To Kill a Mocking Bird*, Atticus Finch famously says to Scout, "You never really understand a person until you consider things from his point of view [...] until you climb into his skin and walk around in it."

How We Can Make a Difference

What we do matters, not just for ourselves, but as a part of that consciousness that has been coming into being, which is why it is so important to make the distinction between living a life that we are forcing, and one that is grown by that Life-Force.

The choice is to either live a life thought up by our minds and willed into action or to live a life driven and impelled by the Life-Force that is within us. To live a life guided by that Life-Force within us is to become a part of evolution. Both the evolution of consciousness, and the evolution of all material things. In this way we are responding to the impulses that come directly from the source of our being rather than the source of our minds.

So, we become that consciousness that brought us into being in the first place, and therefore fulfill the role that each of us was brought into being to play, because we are all here for a different reason, each of us is unique, and with a unique history of circumstances and conditions, and that very uniqueness makes us ideal to express ourselves in a way that only we can.

We are each at the pinnacle of the development of the people that have brought us here. Our parents, our grandparents, and all the situations and circumstances that they went through, and now it is us in the driver's seat. Our time, our place, our lives.

So what do we do with this unique time?

Or, as Mary Oliver puts it in her poem "The Summer Day": "Tell me, what is it you plan to do / with your one wild and precious life?" Do we carve out our own careers? Or do we try to find out why we are really here, and express that? This is where the stance of being actively passive and not being attached to the outcomes comes into play, because your life is not *your* life. It belongs to that greater Life-Force that brought you into being in the first place. And if you are willing to give up your own ambitions, and instead become a part of life's great longing for itself, then you take your place in the unfolding of evolution.

We are all unique parts of that evolution of consciousness. Of life's longing for itself that drives us forward to whatever completion is. Whether you call it the second coming, or something else, that Life-Force is expressing itself from within us, and drawing us to itself from outside us.

I see that completion, that second coming, as the point where the whole world recognizes itself as being a part of one interconnected whole, where the divine in each of us recognizes the divine in each other, and we see the world for what it truly is. Heaven is, in fact, this world truly seen. That point of realization is the point where the world is at peace with itself, and at peace with the creation process. This is what Teilhard de Chardin calls "The Omega Point."

At the moment, we are within time, unfolding ourselves with the unfolding of the Life-Force, and that self-same Life-Force is outside time continually drawing us to itself, to a moment outside time, which, when we arrive, will disappear time itself and show us the nature of the eternal. That is what is meant by eternal life. It is us, in this life, responding to something outside time, and therefore gradually, bit by bit breaking down the idea of time that we are so bound by.

We have a distinct role in this, and that role is to cooperate with that Life-Force, one that is not uncaring, but one that always manifests as the highest possible good. Like water flowing down a stream, this sort of intelligent design always nourishes, always protects, always moves forward. It is latent potential always expressing the highest possible good. A latent love at the center of the universe is unfolding through the evolution of creation, and will eventually take all that is to a perfection that it is always striving to realize. Everything is perfect and we are a part of that perfection.

Our role in life is to be a part of that. To unfold in our own unique way, expressing our own latent potential, always expressing the highest possible good. And what is that highest possible good? Well, it is different for each of us. It is based on our own unique set of circumstances and challenges that have brought us into being in the way that we are. No one else has our challenges, and only we can transform those challenges into the highest possible good, that emotional alchemy.

But to find our way to that is what we are here for. Not to be a success, or to raise a family, or to do better than our parents, but to respond in the most loving way to the circumstances we have in our lives. When we do that, when we fulfill our true potential, rather than the one we dream up in our imagination, then we get to take our place in the story of evolution. Our little bit moves everything forward just a bit, and so inevitably evolution itself moves forward just a bit.

What we do matters. Everything we do matters, because it affects everything else, and you can see it in the story of life. You can see it in the way that society and civilization has gradually developed. Because all the money and power and wealth of Western civilization are not better than all the work and wealth that other civilizations have developed, because wealth is just the ability to appreciate experience.

We are living in a global consciousness now, and it all counts. From the humblest village in Africa to the swankiest apartment in Manhattan, transformation of consciousness happens as people express that highest possible good. And each expression is of equal value irrespective of the material circumstances. Because it is not about the material circumstances, it is about consciousness.

Because that is what evolution is about now. A growth in love and awareness that is the ground of all being calling to itself. Calling to us as the universe now conscious of itself. And our role is to hear that call and act upon it. To live for that Life-Force as living sacrifices. From the Latin *Sacri ficio*, to be literally made holy. So that our lives are given over to the loving process of creation, rather than our own individual whims or concerns. And as we do that, all creation moves toward that eternal moment.

Compassion

We think we have come so far in our civilization, but when Gandhi was asked what he thought of Western civilization, he said, "I think it would be a good idea."

Compassion, from the two Latin words *com* and *passio*, means literally "to suffer with." We have come to a point where we can identify with just those who we feel are on our side; family, friends, and country. This compassion goes beyond that. It takes a worldview. Not what is best for me and my country, but what is best for us and our world. It has to come, and it is better that it comes through a further evolution of consciousness, rather than as a result of some eco disaster.

When we choose that Life-Force to flow through us, we become as one with all things, and we become a part of transformation; no longer preoccupied with our "small self," and small interests, but instead we identify with all, and we feel with all. Our call is a call to transform the world from slavery and bondage to freedom and justice.

You can see people who have done this in the world: Martin Luther King, Gandhi, and Nelson Mandela, who with his famous line when asked if he wanted revenge for all that had been done to him in his life, said: "Do I want revenge, yes—but I want something else more, peace for my country."

Meister Eckhart said, "There is no such thing as 'My bread.' All bread is ours, and is given to me, to others through me, and to me through others. For not only bread, but all things necessary for sustenance in this life are given on loan to us with others, and because of others, and for others, and to others through us."

Through our compassion, our willingness to share pain, we facilitate this because what we do has an effect on those around us. As with the observer in the quantum mechanics experiment affects the position of the electron, so what we do out of our consciousness affects the consciousness of the whole.

We exist in a consciousness of interdependence; we all need each other as unique parts of one community and our compassion is the way that we connect together. It opens the door between us and others, between us and everything else. Eckhart says that "In Compassion, peace and justice kiss." Jesus perfectly sums that up when he invites us to love the others ... as yourself. We open ourselves to feeling for others as we do for ourselves, and therefore we do not cut off from the pain that others sometimes bring us. We feel with that pain.

It is through our openness that we provide the links between people, and through our compassion that we love the world into transformation.

Henri Nouwen said, "Let us not underestimate how hard it is to be compassionate. Compassion is hard because it requires the inner disposition to go with others to the place where they are weak, vulnerable, lonely, and broken. But this is not our spontaneous response to suffering. What we desire most is to do away with suffering by fleeing from it or finding a quick cure for it."

Suffering

That compassion will obviously lead to some personal suffering. In fact, life is painful.

You only have to look at those four noble truths from Buddhism:

> Life has inevitable suffering.
> There is a cause to our suffering.
> There is an end to suffering.
> The end of suffering is contained in the eight-fold path.

And, of course, the eight-fold path involves eight practices: right view, right resolve, right speech, right conduct, right livelihood, right effort, right mindfulness, and right "samadhi." But that is another book!

There's quite a bit of suffering going on in our lives. Scott Peck famously wrote in the opening sentence to his book, *The Road Less Travelled*: "Life is difficult"; and yet we want it to be easy. We do not want to suffer, we do everything we can to NOT suffer.

However, when asked if we want to live a passionate life we say, "Oh, yes!"

The key to this is to recognize that right from the moment we are born our life is *passio*, passion, filled. And we either go with that or we resist it.

Passion and engagement with pain are really a recognition of the creative process. Just look at the nature of birth; you don't get more passionate than that: pain, struggle, and the possibility of ecstasy all rolled into one. When we speak of someone being passionate about their skiing, or their painting, or their work, or whatever it is, we really mean that they are willing to go the distance, to go that extra mile in order to express themselves through that particular pastime. So passionate living is really about the nature of our expression.

As children, we throw ourselves into things, but as we feel pain we begin to learn how to avoid it. First we turn to sweets, then alcohol, then drugs, then shopping, then careers, then righteousness. We begin to bleed the pain out of our lives, just like surgeons in olden times bled their patients because they thought they would get better.

But it only weakened them—we know that now; and so it is with pain and passionate living. The eradication of the pain in our lives leaves us strangely empty. Something is missing, but we cannot put our finger on what.

Khalil Gibran says,

> Your pain is the breaking of the shell that encloses your understanding.
>
> Even as the stone of the fruit must break, that its heart may stand in the sun, so must you know pain.
>
> And could you keep your heart in wonder at the daily miracles of your life, your pain would not seem less wondrous than your joy;
>
> And you would accept the seasons of your heart, even as you have always accepted the seasons that pass over your fields.
>
> And you would watch with serenity through the winters of your grief.
>
> Much of your pain is self-chosen.
>
> It is the bitter potion by which the physician within you heals your sick self.
>
> Therefore trust the physician, and drink his remedy in silence and tranquility:

For his hand, though heavy and hard, is guided
by the tender hand of the Unseen,
And the cup he brings, though it burn your lips,
has been fashioned of the clay which the Potter has
moistened with His own sacred tears.[1]

Controlled by Pain

Pain is an inextricable part in our lives, as well as telling us the places we need to pay attention to in order to heal.

Right from the moment stone age man tried to get himself comfortable in his cave we have been struggling with pain and suffering. It is what banded people together in tribes in the first place. They found that they could share their problems and solve them together. The difficulty came with the development of leaders of those tribes and the exercise of power.

In order to develop and hold onto power, leaders began to use the pain and suffering as a way of exerting control. If you do not do this, then other tribes will attack you. If you do not do that, then you will be uncomfortable in the winter; and so pain and suffering became bound up with community life. When people or individuals felt pain, they tended to look for others to blame that pain on, and so one of the ways out of pain was to transfer that pain onto others. And we do it to this day. Often, the moment we feel any pain we want to blame someone else for it. We complain about how so-and-so is doing such-and-such and how they are bad and wrong. We do it because it makes us feel better, lessening our pain because we have transferred it onto them.

That is what a scapegoat is. We blame others for something that is going wrong. Like a "Jonah" on a ship. Traditionally, it was a goat that tribes would say was causing the problem, and therefore that goat was driven out into the desert and killed.

It works on a personal level, as we blame people we see as doing wrong and doing us harm, making us feel bad.

We also do it on a national level, Jews in Nazi Germany, Muslims, foreigners taking our jobs, war on terror, European bureaucracy, drug lords. We blame them all for our pain, and we go to war to get rid of them. Over the years leaders have seen this and used our pain in order to control us. Feudal lords used the fear of other barbarians to keep their people in line. Landlords who used the fear of famine to force servitude on peasants who felt that they had no option as the only alternative was starvation. The church used the existential fear of God as a way of controlling their followers, as well as the real fear of torture and execution if their beliefs were not followed. For fear of having no work, industrial workers flocked to cities for wages despite the atrocious conditions. Politicians create fear of other countries in order to persuade us to go to war. Fear of the foreigner, fear of the communist, fear of the outsider. All of it is done to persuade the rest of us to conform.

We have now reached a point where fear has become completely industrialized. Instead of experiencing pain, right now the world is containing it. We do that through the use of force, incarceration, military might, and aggression. It is all part of the industrialization of fear. Fear drives much of our economy right now. Fear of "the criminal" is creating more and more people being sent to private prisons that are designed to make money.

The industrial military complex plays on our fear of a lack of security through ongoing war and defense spending that serves to create huge profits for suppliers. Fear of the "terrorist" drives us into giving up our civil liberties and allows for a greater and greater intrusion of the state into everyday life, at the same time boosting the profits of security companies. Fear of one country for another creates world tension that keeps leaders in power and keeps the people servile.

We take our pain and our suffering and we say to our governments, "Tell us who is to blame for the way that I feel. Tell us who is threatening us. Tell us who has taken our jobs. Tell us who is undermining our culture. And in return we will give you the power to take that pain away from us." But, of course, they never do. They give us our scapegoats so that they can direct our anger, and then we are left with some other pain that we have to deal with.

This is that activity that comes from Einstein's first option regarding the universe being a friendly place: "If we decide that the universe is an unfriendly place, then we will use our technology, our scientific discoveries and our natural resources to achieve safety and power by creating bigger walls to keep out the unfriendliness and bigger weapons to destroy all that which is unfriendly and I believe that we are getting to a place where technology is powerful enough that we may either completely isolate or destroy ourselves as well in this process."[2]

That is what is happening with the industrialization of fear, and it happens on a personal level, too. Our emotional pain is someone else's fault. Our economic pain. Our physical pain. So, we blame our spouse, our neighbor, our workmates, our school. Out comes the anger, and the blame is transferred, maybe with words, maybe with guns, or maybe just by blaming them in our heads.

This unwillingness to feel pain is killing our world and our society. While we blame others and try to transfer our pain, we will not heal. Blaming others is so easily done. You feel alone in your marriage, so you take it out on your wife. You feel deprived, so you take it out on your parents. You feel left out, so you take it out on your friends. We all do it.

The great lesson in life is that you have to transform your pain rather than transmit it.

That is the whole lesson of Jesus on the cross. So much has been written about saving us from our sins and all that stuff, that the simple essence is missed. The meaning of the cross is that we are to transform the world by allowing ourselves to feel the pain of the world, without transferring it to others. The power of the crucifixion is that Jesus is wrongly accused, beaten, tortured, humiliated, and killed and he does not complain. He even forgives those who are doing it to him. "Father, forgive them, for they know not what they do." The power of the crucifixion lies in that it shows us how to love. That when we feel pain it has to be transformed, not transmitted. Jesus took the pain and the humiliation and he transformed it. Do not resist an evil person. If someone strikes you on the right cheek, turn to him the other also. He lived out his truth to all who were around him and the transformation came about.

Gandhi said many great things, but two of them are "An eye for an eye makes the whole world blind," and "Be the change you want to see in the world." It is only by seeing things from that perspective that you can make sense of "Love your enemies and pray for those who persecute you." We have to be able to transform our pain, not transmit it to others, who then become mad with the pain and fall into the stereotype we have created for them.

Emotional Photosynthesis

This has implications for all of us. I am suggesting that our role in life is to take what the world offers us, even the pain, and transform that pain within ourselves. And once that pain has been transformed, to respond with love; and that is something that we can call emotional photosynthesis—taking the heat and turning it into love.

Plants take the heat of the sun and turn it into sugar; that is what is known as photosynthesis. It enables carbon dioxide and water to become oxygen, and that gives us life. Huge rain forests all over the world help keep our planet oxygenated. In the same way, we have the capability of taking all those negative emotions—anger, fear, sadness, and taking in the pain that we feel—and giving out love.

Emotional photosynthesis enables us to take pain and not project it out to others, but convert it into love. Like trees, it happens one person at a time, and it is our true role as an evolved human being. That is the process that will enable our planet to be transformed. In fact, that is how world peace will eventually come about. Meeting anger, fear, hatred, pride, and all forms of pain with love is really another way of saying love your neighbor as yourself.

How we transform all forms of pain into love, to take the anger and the grief and the fear and the pride and respond with love, is to give up our agendas, our idols, our long-held beliefs, our virtues, our ideas about how we get it right, and just be open to being led in the moment.

Zen master Robert Kennedy says that "Transformation happens silently and beyond our consciousness."

In other words, we are not really in control of the change that affects us at the deepest point. It is something that goes on quietly in our hearts, and it requires both faith and trust in order for it to happen. This is where personal transformation links to spiritual practice. We are always so quick to respond, but the ability to have our pain and see how we could transform it into love is key to the way we affect the world. You feel pain coming from somewhere and the instinctive response is to blame, to get rid of that pain. But what if you just experienced it, and saw the pain in others that has ended up in you? What if you reflected on the most loving way to respond to your pain?

What if you responded by listening to your wife or husband and holding them? By responding to your neighbor in a way that diffused the problem about the hedge rather than exacerbating it? By not responding to another country's aggression with more aggression?

I was once in a cab with a driver who was so rude that it was beyond belief. At the end of the cab ride I gave him his $20 for the trip, and added an extra $40, thanking him for his service. You should have seen the look on his face.

Where Do We Take Pain to Transform It?

Into our spiritual practice. That is the engine room that allows us to create love in our lives. It is where we bring the divine in, and that turns the base metal of pain into the gold of love. Emotional alchemy.

That is the true nature of the alchemist's task, and the secret meaning of life. Emotional alchemy is living life as an art, where your materials are your thoughts, your feelings, and your emotions. You bring them together in the melting pot of the divine spirit, and the result is an outpouring of love—true passion.

We have to embark on this spiritual practice with a simple trust that we are not in control. That we do not know what will happen. All we can know is that we are responding with love and that if the universe is a friendly place our loving contribution will make some difference. In practice, we are not trying to get anywhere. But we have a faith and a trust that by doing the loving thing, something is slowly and inexorably changing, even if we cannot perceive it. In fact, we should not even try to perceive it because it is not our work to do. We just do the practice and through that transformation happens silently and beyond our consciousness.

That is how the world changes, slowly and inexorably, but imperceivably to the naked eye. Just as we cannot see the mountains form, or the seas divide, so we cannot see our own change. We transform the world by having and transforming our pain—not blaming others for it—but recognizing it as being what we have been given to take on for the sake of others.

Forgive them, for they know not what they do.

Jesus brought love to his pain, and that resulted in his transformation, and so we have to receive the pain we are given and also transform it with love.

Forgive them, for they know not what they do.

And the result will be our small contribution to the reducing of anger and hatred in the world, and the bringing of more love.

Why Bother?

But this all seems like quite a lot of hard work, and it poses the question: Why do I bother to try to be good, to do the right thing?

What difference does it make anyway? And would I not have a much better time of life if I just did what I fancied, rather than trying to do the right thing.

Because to be good or suspend my will and allow the will of that intelligent design to come through, because you can't think yourself good, or become good by doing goodly things, you have to allow goodness to come though at the essence of our being, which just seems like a lot of hard work.

Is it me willing this? Is it that Life-Force? Can't I just get a life and get on with it? I have willingness fatigue. So why do I bother? The ennui of willingness. A sort of tiredness about doing the right thing. So why do we bother with any of it? Not to bother makes life a lot easier. You just have to get by with the least amount of resistance and greatest amount of pleasure. Not quite in a warm bath with headphones on and a TV screen, but pretty close. We could all think of ways of making our lives a lot easier and a lot more pleasurable. So why don't we?

Well, I think the first reason we do not is out of habit. I do things because I have always done them and that is the person who I am. I have always run, so to stop would be a major thing. It is easier just to carry on without thinking about it. I have always meditated. I have always gone to church, I have always tried to be nice to people. To change any of those is to fundamentally change who I am, so it is easier to carry on without really thinking about it.

And so I carry on being in the same sort of way that I have always done, because that is who I am. It is less stressful than continually reassessing who I am and what I should be doing. I float in the current of my worldview. It warms me, it carries me along, and it brings like-minded people close to me who support what I do.

That is another reason why I bother: I care what people think about me. I want them to think well of me. I create a certain way of being and a certain image that fits with the one I have cultivated over the years. And that is a motivation for bothering.

It starts at a very early age. When we are very little we think that we are perfect and that life is perfect. We do not see imperfection anywhere. Our parents coo over us and tell us that they love us, whatever we do, including puking up over them and doing whatever and however we like. We can do no wrong.

Then suddenly, one day, probably at about the age of two, we pick up a crayon and see this huge expanse of whiteness in front of us. Mummy and Daddy always like the pictures that you draw, saying how great they always are, so you decide to do a huge picture for them. You cover the white space in all the colors that you have, making a fabulously creative design.

But when you fetch Mummy and show her what you have done, she reacts with fury. "How could you be so naughty," she shouts, "drawing all over the wall." She gets Daddy and both of them make a lot of noise that seems to be directed at you. And so you have the first dawning realization that things are not all as they should be.

That, horror of horrors, you have done something that is not perfect. In fact, it is more than that. You have the terrible realization that you are not perfect.

You are not perfect, and the world is not perfect. And so you think, or rationalize as only two-year-olds can, and you come up with the next basic question: "If I am not perfect, what must I do to be perfect?" It is logical. You were perfect, now you are not, so how do you go back to perfection? And the answer is there, right in front of you in the shape of your parents.

They told you that you are not perfect, therefore they must tell you how to be perfect. And so you make the fateful decision that will stay with you for the rest of your life:

You do what you think they will approve of.

You begin to seek approval. You do not get it right every time. In fact, sometimes you are so angry about things that you willfully go against their approval (especially in adolescence). But basically you begin to see yourself in terms of the way others see you. You want to please others, because then they are nice to you and life works better.

And so, corruption sets in. You continually try to second guess what you ought to do in life, not using your own experience, but looking to the experience of others. You give away the one real power that you have, the power to act on your life experiences. Over the years you give away power to friends (peer pressure), teachers, religions, groups, governments, gurus; in fact, anyone who can make a case for knowing more about life than you do. Their approval becomes a key motivating factor. And it also leads to the second reason I bother—out of duty.

I bother because I think I ought to. I run because I think I ought to. I do this job because years ago I had a big experience and I think it is my duty to communicate it. I try to be charitable because I think I ought to.

So much of my behavior is about doing what I think it is my duty to do. And that is quite a motivating factor. Are you the same when people are not looking? How good are you when no one is looking? When you can get away with it? Do you get away with it? When no one is looking? And if you do not, how much of that is motivated by a sense of duty?

I find it a powerful factor. So, I bother because "It is what I have always done"; it is a habit. I bother because I care about what others think of me. And I bother out of a "sense of duty." Because it is what I think I ought to be doing. But, to be quite honest, not one of these motivations is particularly edifying.

When it comes down to it, I think the reason I bother is because there is something in life that is demanding that I bother. Not the people out there, not my own reasons, but something that is pulling on my heart. It is as if at some point in my life I opened myself up to a greater will, a greater spirit that is calling me to become involved with life.

The evolutionary thinker Teilhard de Chardin talks about God being in creation, but from a perspective that transcends time. Of God, at some point in the future, drawing the whole universe to greater consciousness through love. And that is the imperative to bother that I relate to. That God is drawing us to Teilhard's "Omega Point."

There is a love that arises in us and connects with a divine love, and that carries us through, if we let it. In going with that love, and responding to it, we become a part of an evolutionary unfolding, that leads toward this Omega Point, this complete unity with God that is at some point in the future, but because God is there and also here, and is drawing us toward it, means that this is already happening, that it has already happened, and that somehow that love is outside time. That eternal love, outside time, is drawing us into a future that is already happening, is the eternal love that Jesus speaks of, and is the ultimate motivating factor for why we bother.

We bother because we cannot help ourselves. We have given a part of ourselves into the keeping of the Divine, and that draws us onward and gives us the motivation, the energy, the umph to overcome. To run up that hill, to do what we do. To meditate, to care, and to bother. Our role is to assent to that when it comes, and to know that it will be OK in the end. To take responsibility for our connection with creation and to play our part in that creation.

It says in Romans 12:

> 1 Therefore, I urge you, brothers and sisters, in view of God's mercy, to offer your bodies as a living sacrifice, holy and pleasing to God—this is your true and proper worship.
> 2 Do not conform to the pattern of this world, but be transformed by the renewing of your mind. Then you will be able to test and approve what God's will is—his good, pleasing and perfect will.[3]

That is the essence of why we should bother, and when we really give up to it, we find it is really no bother at all. It is effortless. It is what we mean by being in the flow of life. Sacrifice—literally made holy. And in allowing ourselves to be "made holy," we flow effortlessly toward that Omega Point, and the way that we do that is to lean into the difficulty when we experience it, and know it is the price we are paying for making our contribution to the transformation of the world. As I run up that hill I feel the difficulty, and I know that I am called to bear that. So I lean into it rather than resisting it.

As we confront the idea of being good, rather than anything else, we lean into it and take up the effort, knowing that this is what we are called to do in our life. It is what gives us meaning, it is what we are here for—and to shirk it is to shirk the reason why we came into being in the first place.

Chapter 4
Living the Life-Force

It is one thing to ramble on about the spiritual life, it is another thing to live it. Spirituality and religion are the easiest thing to talk and argue about, because they are so subjective. But to actually live a spiritually based life is filled with problems.

The words "Who says?" loom large as you try to navigate your way through the rules and regulations that you aspire to follow. Meditate every day, go to your yoga class, be nice to everyone, love your enemies; they are all full of the kind of "shoulds" and "oughts" that would send any sane person running from the spot. On top of that, the idea of being actively passive seems to give no security whatsoever. You just know that the cancer cell within you is poised to go rogue and send you off into a whole different level of forced acceptance.

Is there an attitude, a way that we can be that will put us in the right place to be able to strike the right balance between what we try to do and what we allow to be done to us? How do we cooperate with Einstein's friendly universe? By not getting in the way, and yet not being so passive that we make no difference at all? The only place to start is in the way we experience our lives.

The Big "I Am"

All of us experience life in a position of complete aloneness. As you sit there reading this book there is only you, and there has only ever been you since you were born. There is you, and then there is everyone else who is outside. None of us shares your experience. There is what goes on in your consciousness, and then everything else outside it. That gives us the "I-ness" of our lives. There is only I. And then there is what the "I" perceives.

And here is where the dilemma begins, because the temptation is therefore to live for that I. To nurture it and drive it and build on it so it becomes bigger, more successful, more impactful, more meaningful; and that, of course, is the way we force our lives into the journey that we want to take. Deciding on our destinations, and then driving our lives toward them.

As we look out at the rest of life we compare ourselves to others and make judgments, based upon our own experience, as to who is doing this successfully, and who less successfully. Then we rank ourselves alongside the people we compare ourselves with. And the result is our experience of self-esteem. We judge ourselves by whatever criteria we have thought up, in comparison with others.

That is how we choose to live most of the time; and yet it is possible to see that experience in a different way: To consider the possibility that this experience of "I" is in fact a part of something greater, something that we occasionally get hints of in peak experiences—a greater "I," the Life-Force itself prompting us to become a part of something greater than ourselves. We might catch a glimpse of it in a glorious sunset, or in the most intimate part of a relationship. It is a bigger consciousness that we could possibly be connecting with, and that connection comes through our own sense of "I." When people claim to be having an experience of enlightenment, they are often having a direct experience of that greater conscious. Whereas previously they felt separate, now they feel a part of a greater whole.

When you have that experience, and I talk about my own experience of this at length in my last book (*Developing Consciousness*; see excerpt in the Appendix) you often experience your life as not your own, that you are a part of something greater. This can lead to a desire to give up on your individual wants and needs in order to serve the wants and needs of the greater good.

And here we have the dilemma. Because everything tells me that the "I" that is me, the one that I have always experienced, the one that I know and by which I am known by others, seems to be at variance with this greater I, this greater self.

How do we decide which is right? Which is guiding us? Which should be guiding us?

It says in the Upanishads:

> Like two birds of Golden plumage, inseparable companions, the individual self and the immortal self are perched on the branches of the selfsame tree. The former tastes of the sweet and bitter fruits of the tree; the latter tasting of neither calmly observes.
>
> The individual self, deluded by forgetfulness of his identity with the divine self, bewildered by his ego, grieves and is sad, but when he recognizes the

worshipful Lord as his own true self, and beholds his
glory he grieves no more.

Seeing him present in all the wise man is humble,
puts not himself forward. His delight is in the self, his
joy in the self, he serves the Lord in all.[1]

Our struggle here is being able to make the distinction between
the two. How do we decide when it is the individual self-deluded by
forgetfulness, and when it is the worshipful Lord in all his glory?
Our life can be spent struggling with this dilemma and trying to
humble ourselves and not put ourselves forward, and delighting in
the true self.

There is a story of a monastery. The abbot of the monastery
died and members of the order were asked to say why they should
become the next abbot. A blackboard is erected in the courtyard, and
applicants were invited to submit their ideas. The abbot's deputy,
who was also the favorite to inherit the title, wrote on the board
that the mind is like a polished mirror, and not until every speck
of dust is removed from the mirror will the mind become clear and
enlightenment attained. He then went on to explain the nature of
the mirror and the nature of the speck of dust. The contribution was
admired by everyone for its eruditeness. Then one morning it was
discovered that someone had drawn a line through the whole passage
and simply written "What polished mirror? What speck of dust?"

The head monks immediately launched an investigation to find
out who had done this thing, when they found the man was one of
the cooks. They made him the new abbot. Because the thing that
the cook realized, that no one else had, was that the whole dilemma
of the greater self and the smaller self, of Life-Force or forced life,
is in fact an illusion. There is no dilemma and no decision to make
because the very fact that you make a distinction between the greater
self and the smaller self is an error in itself.

We create the idea that there are two aspects of our self in order
to explain the fact that we experience ourselves as being separate
and distinct from the greater self. They are one and the same thing.

The reality is that it is all one thing, the higher self and the lower
self. There is no fight between the two, there is just a letting go into
what is. The realization that everything is all a part of the same.
This is why in the Upanishads both birds are in the same tree. The
individual self and the immortal self are perched on the branches of
the selfsame tree.

It goes on to say that "the subtle self, within the living and breathing body is realized in the pure consciousness wherein is no duality."

And that is the key bit. There actually is no struggle, because the small self that worries about being successful is actually the same self as the greater self, the Life-Force that is driving everything. We do not have to embark on the struggle, we have to let go of the struggle and let be. We have to see the desires of our hearts and our minds, and know that they are coming from the very same place as the impetus to move toward the greatest good. They both are of one. And we create a struggle by favoring one over the other and thinking that we have to decide. We do not.

In the end all our desires, all our wishes will be fulfilled by a giving up. A giving up to the desire, and a giving up to the fact that we do not have to fulfill that desire ourselves. That is what is meant by "seek first his kingdom and his righteousness, and all these things will be given to you as well." There is only one urge, and that urge is toward the greatest good.

All other urges are merely aspects of that one urge that we misinterpreted and redirect in ways that we think will satisfy those urges, rather than giving those urges into the greater urge toward good. So, as we live our lives we are conscious of our wants and needs. And we judge those wants and needs. Some we judge as good and some we judge as bad, and we act accordingly. We say that is from the small self, and that is from the expanded self, therefore I will do the nobler thing. We have to see that there is no nobler thing. There is just what is. And all of it is a part of the same thing.

Holding All Life in Tension

Now, the upshot of this is that there are in fact no real decisions to be made, there are only what we perceive as options. But those options are not things to be judged and acted upon; they are merely to be held until right action arises.

As Lao Tzu puts it,

> Do you have the patience to wait
> till your mud settles and the water is clear?
> Can you remain unmoving
> till the right action arises by itself?

We have to hold all things within the tension of the one whole. To hold the struggle without taking sides. To see that there are no sides to take and that the struggle is the reality. It is something to be with rather than try to end. In the marriage service, we vow "To have and to hold from this day forward in sickness and in health." We are in fact married to life. Married to the struggle, and our desire to choose one way or the other is simply a way of ending the struggle. Homicide—killing a person, fratricide, killing your brother. Deciding, killing the alternative.

So, our real role in life is to hold all that comes our way in a loving embrace. To see the two birds in the one tree, to recognize our feelings, our wants, and desires and not negate them, but to hold them. To be with the struggle as the very reason for life itself. To have the struggle without pushing it away. This is to live life for the sake of itself.

To be alive is all that we hope for. It brings its own rewards, and you can never predict what they are going to be. You do not hold out for the time that you are enlightened. You know that you already have everything, and you just let it unfold in front of you, realizing that it is never going to be any better than it is right now. And if you can get that, you are home and dry. If you can accept that that which you have now is all of it—and so you might as well enjoy it while you have got it—then you will always be rich.

The reward for sitting in silence is sitting in silence. The reward for mindfulness is mindfulness, the reward for knowing divine consciousness is that divine consciousness; it is as simple as that. Things in life are not better or worse, they are different, and whether you think that difference is better or worse will be a judgment that your mind will make at some point in the future, but outside that—it will just be what it is—right now.

As Khalil Gibran says, "And you would accept the seasons of your heart, even as you have always accepted the seasons that pass over your fields. And you would watch with serenity through the winters of your grief."

It is all here and available, right now. The rest is what you think about it. Real transformation comes when you see "what is" for what it is. That pain is just pain, and joy is joy. They are different. But the really difficult thing is that we do not like being with the difficulty. If we are able to be with the difficult times in the same way as the easy times, then life would be simple and easy in its difficultness. It is about wanting what you get, rather than trying to get what you want. When you do that, you trust life. You trust the hand you have been dealt. You trust your ability to play that hand, and you make no prejudgments about the way the game is going. You are not running the game; life is running it. Work with your life and you have everything you need. The moment you try to take over the game, to change your hand, to change the game, you are lost—because it is not your game, you are a part of a bigger game being played by life.

Practice

In reality, all this is done in practice: In meditation, in yoga, in being in the present, you hold all things without acting upon them. You wait until the mud settles and right action arises by itself. As it says in Romans 9:28: *All things count for good to those that love the Lord.* So we just sit and watch. Wanting for nothing, knowing that all is present and available to us. Willing nothing, knowing that there is nothing for us to do, because we want for nothing. And knowing nothing. Realizing that all our judgments, all our decisions are taken from a partial view, and that we could not ever see the whole picture, and therefore there is no point in trying. Best not to know, but to hold.

All you can do is realize that pure consciousness wherein there is no duality. It is a state of being and a state of mind. Something that we cultivate in meditation, or in quiet times when we can practice the paradox of wanting to make things different, and knowing that they can only be what they are. This practice is actually all of our life's work, if we were but to know it. Whatever calling we have, whatever wonderful career we have developed, the real work is dealing with that paradox and being OK with the way things are compared to the way we think things might have been.

No One Knows Nothing

We then have to ask how any of this makes a difference to anyone else. Surely being dynamic and getting out there to get things done is better than eternally struggling with these paradoxes.

We can think "I'm just an ordinary person. I get on with my life and try to do the best I can, but the idea that I could make a difference on a global scale is laughable. I leave that to politicians, business leaders, gurus, philanthropists, and celebrities. I'm just little old me."

But you know, the funny thing is that if you got into the heads of those politicians, business leaders, gurus, philanthropists, and celebrities you'd find that they think just like you do. If you delved deep down into their thoughts, you would find that they were amazed that they had come as far as they have. They may put on a good show of knowing what's what and being in control, but in reality they go to the toilet, they worry about their kids, they watch ball games, they stress about getting old, and they worry about what others think of them. They might have developed a specific skill set of, say, oratory, or reading balance sheets, or hitting a ball, or copying others, but the rest of their brain works the same way that yours or mine does.

When confronted by a man in tears, they have the same "O my goodness, how do I deal with this?" as a world leader does when they are confronted by another world leader playing at being the bully.

William Goldman, the screenwriter, said of Hollywood, "*No one knows nothing.*" By which he meant that no one really knows what makes a film a success or a failure; and the same is true about life, no one knows nothing. Everyone is just doing what they think might work, and hoping for the best. The president, sitting in the White House with all his aides, is pretty much as likely to get his decisions right as you or me. He is just a bloke that has made it to the White House. That is his job—getting to the White House and staying there. Once there and confronted by the problems of the world, he has about as much chance of solving them as you or I do.

In fact, he might have less, if he is operating from the viewpoint of a dualistic world, rather than seeing the world as all a part of one consciousness. That alone puts him at a disadvantage. It looks like they know better and are more important, but they are not. Deep down they think of themselves like we do—as "little old me"; over the years they have learned to act the part of knowing everything—and we buy it every day.

But, we still doubt ourselves. We think "what have I got to offer?" I've got no great skills, I can't get to the White House or throw a curve ball. In the game of life, I've been dealt a pretty ordinary hand. Each of us has been dealt a hand in our lives, and most of us spend our lives trying to throw in the hand we were given, and get another one. The thing we never figure out is the fact that the game is fixed. We might only have been dealt a pair of fives, but in the game we are playing, a pair of fives is a winning hand. Our pair of fives is a winning hand because it has been given to us to play by that same friendly universe that set the game up in the first place.

We look at what others have, and we say, "If only I had wealth and fame, then I would be able to have everything I wanted." And yet that is almost always not true. You might have been given a hand where the ultimate spiritual and emotional fulfillment in your life comes from being exactly who you are and where you are. In fact, you are the only person who would be able to be content in the situation that you are in, because that is how life works. I am not saying that one should not strive to get on and achieve, to go for excellence, and generally to try and make the best out of our lives. We should all do that. What I am saying is that we should play to the hand we have been dealt, knowing and trusting that it is a winning hand, and if we play it correctly we will get our heart's desire.

I am also not saying that we should not fight to get out of situations that are not supportive, where we get hurt and abused. We should always try to improve our lot. What I am saying is that we do not have to be somebody else in order to make that happen. We have the means within ourselves. You can trust your life. No one else has lived life the way you have. You have a completely unique relationship with that life; with the divine consciousness that has given you birth, with the people and the things that you have connected with, and with circumstances and situations that you are involved with.

So … we have just as good a chance at making a contribution on a grand scale as everyone else. Society tells us that we can't, but if we do not buy that and have a go, we can. You have to follow the promptings in your life. Should I join the book club, should I go running? If you truly seek first what that Life-Force is telling you, rather than try and do it under your own steam, then things will open up for you. Your horizon becomes what life can create through you, rather than what you can dream up and make happen under your own steam.

I love this quote from the Dhammapada, the sayings of the Buddha. He is contrasting the conventional approach to religion, and the one really rooted in the divine.

He says, "*He who goes naked with matted hair, mud-besplattered, who fasts and sleeps on the ground and smears his body with ashes, and sits in endless meditation.*" That is the Indian equivalent of going to church every day, doing good works, and generally being a good person. "He who does all those things, so long as he is not free from doubts," so long as he is resting in his own authority rather than God's, he will not find freedom. "But he who lives purely and self-assuredly, in quietness and in virtue who is without harm or hurt or blame," in other words, he who lives by the promptings of life rather than by his own strength, "Even if he wears fine clothes, so long as he has faith, he is a true seeker."

Dropping the Cruel Knife

Being a person of faith—that is the key thing. It means living life knowing that the universe is a friendly place, and that whatever happens, the divine nature is there for you. That is why we do not have to worry about being "up to it," because it is not we who are doing it—it is life, it is all out there, ready for us to walk into, so long as we are innocent enough to recognize it, rather than try to make it conform with our own expectations. We don't know what will happen, or what it will look like, we just sense that something is happening, and we can choose to declare that we are up for it. That is why we can say with confidence, "If not me, who? If not now, when?"

There is that famous story from Haifiz:

> Once a young woman said to me, "Hafiz, what is the sign of someone who knows God?"
>
> I became very quiet, and looked deep into her eyes, then replied, "My dear, they have dropped the knife. Someone who knows God has dropped the cruel knife that most so often use upon their tender self and others."

That, as Bede Griffiths puts it:

> The goal of each religion is the same. It is the absolute, transcendent state, the one Reality, the eternal Truth, which cannot be expressed, cannot be conceived. This is the goal not only of all religion, but of all human existence—whether they like it or not, all men and women are continually attracted by this transcendent Truth. The intellect, in and beyond every formulation by which it seeks to express its thought, is in search of the Absolute. It is made for Being itself, for Truth, for Reality, and it cannot rest satisfied in any partial truth, in any construction of the human mind. It is always being carried beyond itself to the ultimate Truth.[2]

We have become aware of this absolute truth that each of us is a part of.

As the Upanishads puts it:

> IN THE HEART of all things, of whatever there is in the universe, dwells the Lord. He alone is the reality.

And the Tao Te Ching:

> Approach it and there is no beginning;
> follow it and there is no end.
> You can't know it, but you can be it,
> at ease in your own life.
> Just realize where you come from:
> this is the essence of wisdom.

Radical Equality

We are at that point in the evolution of consciousness where we are able to realize ourselves as an expression of the one consciousness that created all. That each of us has within us that same divine spark that was in the big bang, in Buddha, in Jesus, in Muhammed, in Lao Tzu, in Moses. We are that; and not only are we that, but we are all that equally. Everything in the world is equal. However, the direct perception of this equality is blocked by our mental constructs. In other words, our insistence on naming this or that. Of us saying it is so. In reality, we are all equal. You, Christ, Donald Trump, Buddha, Hillary Clinton, Theresa May, the Dalai Lama, Mother Theresa … in reality we are all the same.

Now I know it is difficult to get a handle on, but we see others as more powerful than ourselves just because we conceive it that way. We have been told the story, and we tell the story to ourselves and others that makes out that I am "little old me" here, and Jesus is mighty and over there. But in reality, we are all equal. We are all uniquely an expression of the divine, and we all play our role in the development of the whole. No role is greater or more important than any other. No one planet is more important than any other; that the element potassium is no more important than mercury. Get rid of bees and see how the world would work. No one of us is any more important than any other one of us. And so … what you do matters. Your consciousness and the way you express it matters; not only that, but it has an effect on the whole. We do not know how or why or when. But it does.

Look at the Terminator. Sarah Connor did not realize she was important until Arnie came crashing in from the future and told her that the world depended on her son surviving. Now I may have lost a few of you non-Terminator fans, but I hope you see the point. Who is to say that in three hundred years' time your descendants might have invented a way of bringing world peace, or whatever. You never know. You don't know what you don't know, and one of the things we don't know is how we matter. Mao was once asked what he thought of the French Revolution and he answered, "It is too early to tell."

I like that idea of being told that I am the one who will welcome the Messiah. Well, in my own mind that means me going out and shaking his hand and saying, "Hi, Messiah, welcome to my house." However, in reality, I might just be the doormat that he walks over with the word "welcome" on it. Or the door frame. Or the cushion on the chair that she sits in. We do not know our role. All we have to know is that all lives matter. And that ours matters as much as anyone else's, because we are a part of that divine consciousness just as much as anyone or anything else is.

So what we do matters, and how we are being matters, and whether we are kind or not matters, because it is all feeding into that greater consciousness that we are a part of. Your space, your life matters. And so, we need to treat our lives as if they do. Our meditation is important, how we treat others is important, that we practice emotional photosynthesis is important, that we recognize that there are no others is important. Because we are each of us a part of the evolution of consciousness. But it goes further than that. The idea that there is only you. You being the only person that really exists. You are it. And we are all out here. You contain all of us.

It is a bit like *The Truman Show*. All of us out here are really just extras in your life. We pass by, we say hi, we chat, we come around. But in reality, everything is in your life. You are the consciousness that holds it all. You hold all of us, all of the world, including ISIS, all of space, all of the planets. They are happening within your consciousness. So, in some way, all of us experience ourselves as being the center of the world. We are the sun around which everything else orbits. And yet we convince ourselves that this is not true. That the pope is much more important than we are, as is Bernie Sanders. We have convinced ourselves that what we do does not matter, when in reality that is not our experience!

Our experience is that we are the center of the world.

Now I am not suggesting that we should all go around dictating to "our world" what should happen, although mad people do that.

What I am suggesting is that in reality we know that we can have an effect on our world, and that we do. The question then is still, what do we do?

And the answer is nothing. To have an effect, there is nothing that you have to do. You just have to show up. As Mother Theresa said, "Just show up and things will happen." That is all you have to do, and most of us don't even do that. We think, we hide, we avoid, we are not present. Being present is showing up, and it is your actual presence that facilitates the transformation of the world.

Your presence allows the reality of consciousness to shine through. That consciousness will do the rest. Rely on nothing, so that nothing can do its work.

That great Buddhist quote: "O seeker! Rely on nothing until you want nothing."

Anything else is the ego trying to control, and that creates the separation and naming. A virtue that does not discriminate.

Our role is to be present, to have our presence felt, and to know that it matters. That the work we put into it does and will bear fruit. And that fruit is the fruit that will heal the world.

Whose Life Is It Anyway?

Although we have the illusion of us passing through time, really time is passing through us. Our consciousness is always in the present, and like a surfer on a board, we are still, in the present. The changes we see around us we experience as time, when in reality we are always here in the present, going nowhere. So, we have to take a look at our lives and what we choose to do with the time we are given.

On the personal level, there is a journey of unfolding realization. To take responsibility for our suffering and transform it rather than projecting it out. To take responsibility for our connection with creation. To allow love to arise within us and unify us with all that is around us. We have to become mystics as in Evelyn Underhill's definition: "Mysticism is the art of union with reality. The mystic is a person who has attained that union in a greater or lesser degree; or who aims at and believes in such attainment."

The journey to our own personal fullness of time is the journey toward the realization that heaven is not some otherworldly place, but the world clearly seen. As Paul says in 1 Corinthians 13: "For now we see through a glass, darkly; but then face to face: now I know in part; but then shall I know even as also I am." Each of us is an unfolding consciousness that in flowering offers a pollen of transformation to others in the world that they too might undertake their journey and be fertilized by our experience.

Because as we flower, so others flower in our wake. There is that famous story of the 100th monkey. Monkeys were observed eating sweet potatoes by a lake. The sweet potatoes were covered in grit, and then one young monkey began to wash the potatoes. Soon other young monkeys were doing the same, but the rest of the tribe just carried on eating the gritty potatoes—until the 100th monkey started to wash the potato. And at that point something changed in the colony's consciousness, and then all the monkeys adopted this technique, and always washed their potatoes.

We are like those monkeys in our journey into the fullness of our own time. What we do is like a monkey washing the sweet potato. In the end, everyone will learn. And that is how we participate in the transformation of consciousness.

And it also works on a macro level. The fullness of all time.

From the big bang 13.7 billion years ago, to the universe, to life, to the universe conscious of itself, to the universe conscious of the divine within. All through this process the universe is being drawn to greater consciousness through the inherent love within the system drawing everything into itself. That is the process of creation. Of love drawing us out of ourselves atom by atom into union with itself. And that process is undertaken by evolution. A greater complexity in all things coming together—like all the atoms, minerals, and life within our bodies framing the whole which is a human being. Simple in its appearance but immensely complicated in its construction.

That greater complexity brings unity and wholeness, like the unity and wholeness demonstrated by television, media, and the Internet. A hugely complex system brings about a simple whole. Evolution.

Evolution occurs as consciousness "awakens" from unconscious matter to self-conscious matter. Teilhard de Chardin says, "There is a fundamental energy at the heart of evolution that has two dimensions: the energy within associated with individual consciousness, and the energy without which he associated with tangential energy or love."

Evolution is a process of deepening love and consciousness; that is, as love deepens, consciousness rises.

Teilhard spoke of love as the very definition of existence. To be, is to be with in such a way that what "I am" is what "I love" and what "I love" shapes what "I do"—and what I do is what "I become."

And as these two processes—inner and outer—come together we are being drawn to Teilhard's Omega Point. If the Alpha Point is the Big Bang, the Omega Point is that moment of full consciousness with the divine. When all of this and the divine are conscious of themselves as one. It is that moment when, through the consciousness that is love, we are not all looking at one another but all looking in the same direction. That coming together of all things, an advent, an arrival, coming back to the place where it all started, a oneness with the divine. A second coming. And you know, the amazing thing is that all of it is happening right now.

It is all happening in this present space. Now. But because we are not conscious of it yet we cannot realize it. Those crazy cults that go around saying the end of the world is coming on such-and-such a day are in fact right. But they are too crazy to realize it. You have to be completely sane and present and conscious and loving to realize it. And I am not talking about parallel universes or anything weird. I am actually meaning right now. Because right now is the only place it can happen. We just haven't realized it yet. We probably will at our deaths, because that is another way we experience the fullness of time. But it's much better to get it now.

And why don't we? Because we are not ready. Because the game is not over. Because we are part of something that is 13.7 billion years old and a known universe that is 28 gigaparsecs large. That is 93 billion light-years in diameter. And here are we thinking that we can work it all out. And we can't. And it is not our job to work it out.

I've been spouting off in this book now, but the reality is that I haven't a clue. I don't know what this is all about. I don't know what happens when I die, I don't even really know why I am here. It is all guesswork. And it always has been. Religions are really just the best guess of civilizations over the centuries. Even scientists are dealing in best-guess scenarios. They just try to find out what works, and then give the best explanation as to why it works. And Newton's guesses were very different from Einstein's.

The real question is simply "How can we live our lives more skillfully?" I think that is the purpose of religion. Why something works—we can only guess at. Is it because we are covered in the blood of Christ? Or because we are flowing with the Tao, or because we can understand the sound of one hand clapping? That is our guesswork? Worse, it is our made-up guesswork. Because it is not up to us to know. We just do not have the capacity to know. We are not conscious enough yet. And so, given this time, right now, what do we have the capacity for? What can we know? And how do we respond to what we know? That will give us a pointer as to where to go and what to do.

We have to know that spiritually we want for nothing. We are alive, we are conscious, we are capable of receiving all that life has to offer. And if we want for nothing, then there spiritually is nothing that we need to change, we just need to be with what comes our way and respond to it as deeply as we possibly can—measuring that with our capacity to experience joy. And lastly we have to be willing to not know. We have to give up trying to work out what is going on, and let go into the joy of just being. Meister Eckhart's idea of the meditative state being "Wanting for nothing, willing nothing, and knowing nothing."

And so, in this present moment Heaven and Earth come together in us with the appearance of what we see as time, but in actuality it is just the nature of our being. We want to know why. We want to know what is next. But it is not in our nature to know that. Our nature is not made to know, it is made to love. That is the tool we have been given to participate in the process of evolution and creation. To love. To take in pain and to give out love. Like fish who swim in the sea, we swim in love. We are given that love. And it is given to us to know that love. But like fish not knowing the height or the length or the breadth of the sea, we are not given to know the height or the length or the breadth of life. We just swim in it, we sense its currents, we participate with it. It feeds us, it gives us life, and maybe that's enough.

We are not given to know more. And so, what about the idea of being enlightened? The idea of an awakened consciousness, being a Christ-like Buddha-like, Bodhisattva turning water into wine, healing the sick, and transcending the limitations of this earthly life? Well, the trouble with talking about enlightenment at this level is that you have to be enlightened at that level, and I personally do not experience my life on that level. In fact, I have never met anyone who has. I have read the stories, and I can see the truth in them. But that just is not my reality. And I think when you are looking at the nature of consciousness, all you can really do is to tell the truth about what you do experience. It does not help to try and be where you are not. And that also goes for so-called experiences of enlightenment.

They are really just peak experiences and are no more special than any other experience. The soil at the top of the mountain is the same soil you find at the bottom of the mountain. The only difference is one of perspective. The so-called peak experience is just the same experience as we are having right now. Both experiences contain information relevant to the understanding of reality. It is the same information that enables you to have a sense of perspective about where you are and what is going on right now as you are reading this book.

So, these peak experiences are simply another way of perceiving where you are and what is going on. It is just one way of receiving an information download. The experience of where you are now is a combination of what you directly experience and what you have been told. You experience the place you are in, you know you are on planet Earth, and you have been told that the earth is round, is part of a universe that includes many galaxies, and is about 13.7 billion years old.

What we know comes partly from direct experience and partly from shared knowledge. Consciousness—con-scios, to know with. To know with direct experience, and to know with others. We are aware of racial consciousness, and gender consciousness because we have talked about it as a society. And it is the same with these peak experiences. They are about information, and some of the information can be experienced directly, and some we can be told about. We don't have to go into space to know that the world is a blue planet and that the moon has no atmosphere and less gravity; we have been told that, and all the information we have received agrees with that. Similarly, we do not need to have a direct experience of the interconnectedness of all things. That experience might come our way, but just like going to the moon, a lot of the facilitation of that experience is out of our control. We can get good at math, train to be a scientist, and become an astronaut, but that does not mean we will go to the moon. Similarly, we can meditate and be spiritual, but it does not mean we will have one of those peak experiences. That astronaut knows about the moon because he has been told about it, and it is just not his role to go there himself.

We can know about the interconnectivity of all things and the greater self, but it just might not be us that will experience it. But everything else conspires to tell us that it is true. It is just information, no matter how you receive it. So do not think that awakened consciousness is just about walking around like Jesus or Buddha; it is not. It is you being you in the you-ness of your life. And for you this is it. Do the practice, open yourself in every way you can, and then just get on with it. That is what I do ... trust ... assume ... let it go, until I am brought up short, and then I learn and adapt. The Dalai Lama was asked what he would do if he found out that reincarnation did not exist, and he said, "I would change my views accordingly." Work out for yourself what is true and live by it. You cannot do any more. And, the great news is that you don't have to get enlightened. One less thing you have to achieve! Because it is all here, right now.

Just know it. Heaven is this world clearly seen. That is what it means to live in awakened consciousness.

Furthermore, it is worth remembering that awakened consciousness does not get you to the meaning of life, it *is* the meaning of life. Because there is nothing more to know or to be than awakened consciousness. It is in being fully awakened that you fulfill your purpose in life. It is a resonating whole that unites mind and heart into the true nature of our existence. And it is here that we transform the wantingness and neediness of Eros, of erotic love, into the settled unitive consciousness of Agape, divine love. Love of God for man, and man for God.

As T. S. Eliot puts it at the end of the *Four Quartets*:

> We shall not cease from exploration
> And the end of all our exploring
> Will be to arrive where we started
> And know the place for the first time ...
> ... And all shall be well and
> All manner of thing shall be well
> When the tongues of flames are in-folded
> Into the crowned knot of fire
> And the fire and the rose are one.[3]

Part 2
In Practice

Chapter 5
Some of My Mess

Books like this seem to be written by people who have their lives "sorted." You don't hear how they have to deal with the day-to-day problems that beset the rest of us: chaotic family life, financial challenges, health issues, and all the things that go to make up a normal person's life. People who write spiritual books seem to be above that.

But the very fact that we are not in control means that most of us are always dealing with one sort of mess or another. No one is above all that. So we are really only getting half the picture from books like this. We get the theory, and a bit of insight, but generally not what it is like to be that person, to get a sense of the struggles and mess that they have to deal with on a day-to-day basis.

What follows now is some of my mess: Parts of my life that hopefully will give a window into how I have struggled with some of the issues that are in this book. Of course, it will only be a partial view, but it might give you some idea of who is sitting above the keyboard.

It is a partial memoir, and so as to link it into the issues from the first part of the book, I have reflected on the different levels of consciousness that I described in the first chapter: Infant, Magical, Mythical, Rational, Visionary, and Soul Consciousness.

As I said earlier the story of movement through these levels of consciousness is really the story of decreasing narcissism. A child starts its life, quite properly, completely absorbed with itself. It needs to be that way in order to survive. Gradually it emerges out of that to take in the rest of the world and work out how to interact with it, eventually considering whether or not there might be such a thing as a Life-Force, and how to cooperate with such a thing, if indeed it does exist.

Narcissism is self-centeredness arising from failure to distinguish the self from external objects, either in very young babies or as a feature of mental disorder. Someone describes the definition of a bore as "someone more interested in himself than in me." And that really links in with what we are talking about here.

Throughout our lives, if we have developed at all, it has been with us becoming less fascinated with ourselves and more fascinated with others. As we develop we learn that there is another world out there. We gradually progress through these levels of consciousness, but we also blip in and out of them at different times. We may primarily exist in one stage, yet move into other levels at different times. Maybe we operate at a visionary level in our spiritual lives, but then when it comes to our money, we become very rational.

We move through these levels of consciousness by having realizations about life. We will be living at one level of consciousness, and then have an inner realization about that level. Say, for example, we are living at a rational level, and we have an inner realization, that although rationally it works for us to accumulate money for ourselves, we see others less able to do that than ourselves. We have an inner realization that we could do more for others.

We then make a deduction that this is something we ought to do, and we let go of our "rational consciousness" and instead move into a more visionary way of looking at life, thereby entering "visionary consciousness"; and that process continues throughout life as do realization, deduction, letting go, further realization, and so on. There is no morality about these levels of consciousness. They are not good or bad, they are just what is so. They inform us as to the extent we let go into that Life-Force, or we try to make our own way.

What follows is some reflection as to how I have struggled with my life in relation to these levels, and how they have affected the decisions I have made about making my life work the way I wanted to, as opposed to letting go and allowing the Life-Force to take me.

Chapter 6
Gimme Gimme Gimme

Infant Consciousness

It seems to me that I have lived most of my life in infant consciousness. That first stage in a child's life where they have trouble differentiating themselves from their primary source of food and sustenance, their mother. This leads to an all-inclusive selfishness that really is just looking for "me and mine." Abraham Maslow set out a hierarchy of needs that we all move through: the basic needs of food, water, shelter, and safety; the psychological needs of intimacy, friendship, self-esteem, and accomplishments; and the need to self-actualize, realize our potential, and be creative.

Infant consciousness is about getting "mine," by whatever means, because *I* need it to survive. My earliest memory is of wanting food. Picking wild strawberries from my grandmother's garden. And so much of my life has been about trying to get fed. Our house was always just the three of us, myself, my brother, and my mother. My father died when I was two.

I have no memory of him, just pictures and stories. He was an army officer and died of a cerebral hemorrhage while on active service in Germany. Immediately after his death, the commanding officer of the regiment came around to our house to commiserate with my mother. I had obviously missed my father, and upon seeing the khaki trousers of his uniform I rushed forward, shouting, "Daddy! Daddy!" gripping the familiar-colored trouser legs with my two-year-old arms. Looking up earnestly at what I took to be my father returning, I thereby reduced the commanding officer to tears.

The army had always been a part of our family life and by right I should have gone in myself. I was third-generation army. Both my grandfathers were soldiers. One served in the Boer war, the First World War, and the Second World War. My father was a gunner and served in Africa. My uncle and my mother were both in Mi6 (British

Military Intelligence). I went to school at Wellington College, the feeder school to Sandhurst, the British military academy.

The nearest I got was when I was invited to one of the military "Hunt Balls" held at Sandhurst. I was nineteen. These are huge affairs with an orchestra playing waltzes, officers in uniform, girls in their best dresses, elaborate dances in circles and lines, plenty to eat and drink, and light sparkling from every chandelier. The scene would not have been very different at the dance held in Belgium on the eve of the Battle of Waterloo. It was an impressive sight. Later, I was approached by a couple of officers who invited me outside for a smoke. "Well," they said, "having a good time?" I was slightly overwhelmed by it all as I stood there in my ill-fitting dinner jacket hired for the occasion. I mumbled some form of assent. "Well, how do you fancy joining us? I think you'd fit in well." That was the way they recruited in those days. The king's shilling was pressed into your hand while you were entranced by the glamor of it all. I took in the scene. It looked so attractive, the comradeship, the frivolity, the girls, and I was tempted. But then I had a strange moment of clarity. Despite all of this I was very clear that I did not want to get shot at. And despite all that was in front of me now, the reality of being in the army is that eventually you will end up in someone's sights; and that moment of lucidity made up my mind for me.

It was not that I was against killing others or anything political about the nature of army life. There was no debate about the rights and wrongs of military might. I just did not want to get shot. Cowardice? Probably. Self-survival? Definitely. I was in a generation in England that has never been called on to fight, and for that I feel very fortunate. The years 1850–1950 must have been a nightmare to live through.

This decision set me on a course that took me away from the concept of service that was so embedded in my family, and into a much more open question of what I wanted in my life. To begin with it was the basic needs of attention and love. We were a family that lived together separately, my mother, my brother, and me. We all had our separate needs and we all tried to meet them our own way. Love really went out of the window with the death of my father, and it was a case of each to his or her own. I yearned for touch, for intimacy, for friendship, and for love. But I settled for attention. My behavior was dysfunctional, pushing the limits of what I could get away with at home and at school.

I tried to set fire to the garage doors, I ate weed killer, I put nails under my mother's car tires. I got into fights. I argued with my brother. I was totally lost. I had no way of communicating how

I felt, or what I wanted; so, I just did what I thought would get me attention. That seemed to be the best way to escape the pain of aloneness. There was me, and then everybody out there, which is a characteristic of infant consciousness. I did not consider what other people might be feeling, or what they wanted, it was all about me.

It was not consciously thought out; not an intentional thing; not premeditated. I had a lack of awareness of the needs of others. In my mind, everybody out there had one use, and that was to make me feel better. They were to be used to get what I wanted: food, toys, attention, and proximity to anything, because I felt so distant. And then, at the age of nine, I was sent away to boarding school.

I ended up fat and unpopular and one hundred miles from home, a recipe for psychological disaster. It was an environment controlled by violence. The masters beat you if you broke the rules. The other students beat up on you if they felt like it. Everyone was out of control, like an organized version of *Lord of the Flies*. It was a world of emotional chaos: Most of the masters had just survived the Second World War and were in their own personal hell, and the children were just coping the best they could. There were gangs, codes of behavior, ritual punishment, and constant humiliation. I lived in a maelstrom of violence. Desperately unhappy and always on the lookout for the next attack, I was without safety or sanctuary.

At home, it was impossible to talk about it. One world did not sit easily in the other, and so I just endured. How could they understand what was going on? In the same way that people coming back from war cannot talk about what they have endured, I was living through my own version of trauma. I went deeper into myself. Still alone. Still with the world "out there," but by now I had given up any idea of using the world to get what I wanted and instead became embattled.

Being so out of control I could see no way of making things better. My sole aim was to survive. Amazingly I never even considered running away. It did not even cross my mind. I accepted the world I had been placed in completely, as if fate had placed me there and I had no right to change it.

And that was characteristic of the first thirteen years of my life. I was totally powerless. Even if I wanted to make my own way I was incapable of having the slightest impact on the forces that controlled everything around me. Home and school were both environments that rendered me powerless. All I knew was that I was constantly moving from fear to grief and back to fear again. I could not even be raised to anger, so fast was the hold that fear and grief held me in.

I would begin in fear, terrified as to what drama was going to happen next. It could be a fight, an all-out attack from a gang of boys, being beaten by a master, being humiliated, being hospitalized. All of those things happened often. Actually, I was only hospitalized once, and that was from a punch to my back. I was so worried about telling anyone what had happened that they diagnosed me with a serious case of wind. Then, when a drama did occur I would be reduced to tears, from the pain, from the humiliation, from the aloneness. My realization was that this could not continue.

This came to me suddenly and out of a particular incident. Every weekday evening the whole school came together to do their homework in a series of classrooms loosely supervised by a master who would wander around to make sure nothing untoward happened. This particular evening, I was working on an essay with other boys all around me, when suddenly I was hit on the back of the neck, a karate chop delivered by the boy who was sitting directly behind me, for no other reason than it was fun and would create amusement for those he was sitting with. My response was the usual one. I looked around with indignation and then got on with my work without making any fuss, because I knew that more fuss would create more trouble. I was surrounded by muted laughter.

The next day I was called up in the class for my work to be reviewed. The master called each of us up in turn while the rest of the class got on with something else, so it was a private conversation. It began with the master putting his hand on the back of my bare leg. They did a lot of that in those days, and nobody paid much attention to it. We did not even think about it. "This is a pretty good effort," the master said. "Well done. But what are those watery blotches all over the page? Did you spill something on it?" They were tears. And I saw in that moment that my tears were getting in the way of me achieving anything in life, that my emotions were preventing me from moving on.

Emotions are supposed to move us on from one experience to the next. The word comes from the Latin words *ex* and *movere* to move out. But for me they were doing the opposite. They were a prison. I was trapped by them. I could not escape from being incapacitated by what they were making me feel. Looking at that piece of work, and seeing the tears on the page, I realized the extent to which I had become trapped. And in that moment, I resolved to do something about it. And that something was to stop crying.

I consciously made the decision to bury my emotions, to push them down into myself so I did not feel them so strongly. Instead of waiting for the next onslaught, I learned to read a room. I could tell where the attention was going, and if it looked like it was coming in my direction I learned to deflect it elsewhere: I'd make a joke or point out some fault in others. As a result, I found myself able to avoid the feelings that had so overwhelmed me. And it worked. After that decision, I stopped crying. And to this day I have not cried since.

That, of course, has brought a whole set of other problems in my life, but that was the first time I actually took control. I still did not fight back. In fact, every time I have been physically attacked in my life I crumpled up and offered no resistance. And that seems to work too. But something shifted. I went through the process of having the realization, making a deduction, letting go of my emotions, and moving on to another level. It is how I moved out of infant consciousness and into magical consciousness at the age of thirteen.

At my next school, which was also a boarding school, I coped better. I was sullen and still alone. I was still occasionally victimized, but I now had a reserve that enabled me to withstand whatever came my way. But that infant consciousness stayed with me through most of my life. It resided in the scar tissue left by the abandonment of my emotional life.

Not being willing to cry left a part of me isolated inside. It left a part of me unavailable. And to compensate for it I developed a hunger for touch that plagued me for the first forty-five years of my life. When you fail to put oil into a car it overheats, and when you do not access your emotions it creates a pain that also leads to overheating. There was a pain inside me that needed to be quenched. And, if I was not prepared to cry, then touch was the only way that this pain would go away.

My sexual relationships were not about sharing intimacy, but about pain management. And my desperation led to me developing dysfunctional relationships that never lasted. I was not sharing, I was taking. That drove most people away.

I was lucky that I did not really like the taste of alcohol, and so never tipped into addictive behavior in that area. I did like smoking pot, and for a while I used it as pain management; however, I soon realized that it was not a sustainable way through. It was too expensive, debilitating, and developed a pain of its own that also needed to be dealt with. What saved me from this consciousness, what ultimately moved me on from infant consciousness, was the realization of the existence of that Life-Force. I began to see that the only thing that was going to move me out of this infantile behavior was something that was beyond myself.

Plato's observation (loosely translated) that one's libido was "like being chained to a lunatic for fifty years" applied doubly when that libido was accelerated by pain. And so, at the age of forty-three

I gave up trying to compensate for the pain. I decided to let go of my desire to change the pain and to let it be. To not keep looking for a way out, but to trust that there would be another way provided for me. If that meant never marrying, never being able to develop real intimate relationships, so be it.

I stopped looking. For the next woman. For *the* woman. For any woman. And I just let it be. I saw that in the past I had been going around in circles. That my attempting to deal with the pain through being touched, through therapy (and I'd had plenty of that too), through any substance, was not going to work. In fact, it hobbled me. It turned me in on myself and took me nowhere. So, I gave up and I let be: open to the idea that there was a Life-Force that would take me to that place where I could be healed.

It meant facing that pain on a daily basis. Not trying to get rid of it, but opening myself to a new horizon that I was not yet aware of. And it worked. Something shifted in me, and within five years I was married with a child on the way. It is still a work in progress. I sometimes still feel the pain of aloneness. I have not allowed myself to cry and that makes me unavailable at some level. And yet something inside me has moved on. I am no longer plagued by that insistence to "get mine" that is so characteristic of infant consciousness. I can now feel it when that tendency arises, and I can see that to indulge it will not serve me.

What freed me was the ability to recognize that I could not force my way through life any longer. I could not continue to repress my emotions and cope with the pain that came with that repression. Instead, I gave up to a Life-Force within me, trusting that it would take me to a place that I could not get to on my own. It was a subtle shift, that actually took years to come into effect, but it made me take my hands off the steering wheel, and for the first time really let life take its own course.

A Blessing in Disguise

2001

I woke up on my wedding day with four hours to kill before I was due at the altar.

How do you prepare yourself? A drink was out of the question at 9 o'clock in the morning, I did not really want to face my family, so I decided to go out for a walk.

I left the hotel and headed for the local park. It was quiet at that time with no one around.

I wandered with my thoughts. How had I got to this day? How had I imagined it in the past? Had I thought it would ever arrive?

Eventually I came upon a park bench and sat down.

There was a peace that reflected what I felt in my heart.

Then, out of the corner of my eye I saw someone coming toward me, a shabbily dressed man clutching a bottle of some sort.

He stumbled on his way and had obviously been drinking.

My heart sank. The last thing I wanted was to be disturbed. I braced myself for the encounter.

"Morning!" he said and sat down on the bench next to me.

An odor of sweet decay enveloped me as he took a pull from the bottle.

We sat together for a few minutes. Nothing was said. I realized I had brought no money with me so would not be able to give him anything if he asked for it.

Eventually he broke the silence.

"Nice day!" he said.

I agreed.

Another silence.

"Doing anything interesting today?" he asked.

"Well, er, actually, I am getting married this afternoon," I replied.

He turned his face toward me and I could see that his cheeks were blackened with dirt and the sun, but his eyes were as sharp as stars.

"You know," he said, "getting married is a greater step than Armstrong took when he walked on the moon for the first time. It involves every part of you giving yourself in every way."

I was slightly stunned by this insight coming from such an unlikely source and mumbled some sort of agreement.

"I'd like to give you a blessing," he carried on, "you are going to need all the help you can get."

Now I was really taken aback.

Of course, I could not refuse.

He stood up and walked around behind me and in the full view of the whole park placed his hands on my head.

"May the God of heaven and earth bless you and help you," he began and went on in a similar vein a few minutes. Eventually he stopped. Removing his hands from my head he came around and faced me.

"Well," he said, "must get on. Plenty to do today. All the best with your wedding," and he shuffled off up the hill, still clutching his bottle.

I was left on the bench speechless.

It was as if an angel had arrived in disguise, and, on behalf of all creation, given me his blessing.

Chapter 7
The Age of Aquarius

Magical Consciousness

I cannot say that I have ever been particularly superstitious. I can remember thinking that if I managed to walk on the sidewalks without touching the lines I would pass my exams; however, beyond that, the number 13 holds no fear for me. I can walk under ladders, and I don't feel the need to bless people when they sneeze.

The first time I thought that the world might be actually speaking to me personally was when I heard the album *Strange Days* by The Doors.

For me music has always been a way to feel that connectedness with everything else, to feel that there were other people out there who felt the same way I did. Up till then, it was very much a "me" and "everything else" situation. Nicholas *Contra Mundum*, "Hearing Strange Days," broke through that. I was thirteen, and for the first time it seemed that the world spoke back to me: There were other people who felt the way I did.

Up till then, music was merely a soundtrack. The first album I ever bought was the Beatles' *Hard Day's Night*, and both the Beatles and the Rolling Stones provided music to get by with; hummable, pleasant, and a foot-tapping backdrop. But "Strange Days" was something different. And music became a way of identifying a connection.

I moved from there to the King Crimson's "Court of the Crimson King," "Tommy" by the Who, and finally fell into Pink Floyd's "Meddle," "Atom Heart Mother," and "Obscured by Clouds." I connected with something in each of them, and they opened up the possibility of seeing life in a different way. Seeing the musical *Hair* live on stage in London in 1970 also had an impact. I sensed an alternative way of living, one that acknowledged the pain and rebelled against the way the world was constructed to inflict that pain. There seemed to be a way out that challenged the immovability of the status quo, and those that listened to the music seemed to agree.

I can remember preordering *Dark Side of the Moon* and picking it up from the store the day it came out. The first concert I ever went to was Pink Floyd live at Earl's Court in London in 1973. They began by playing "Set the Controls for the Heart of the Sun," and various bits from "Ummagumma" and "A Saucer Full of Secrets." Then they went off for ten minutes and came back and played the whole of "Dark Side of the Moon" from start to finish. The audience went mad, clapping and cheering for fifteen minutes. Then the band came back and played "Echoes" from Meddle. I left that concert thinking that I would never see one as good, and to this day I have not.

In 1974 I can remember writing a letter to the Wembley Arena Box Office and explaining that I would like tickets to see the Rolling Stones, and when I got the tickets, someone had kindly given me second row seats. Things like that seemed magical, magical in that we were all in some way "in it together."

In London in the 1970s it was possible to see anyone. I can remember getting in line for twenty-four hours to buy Bob Dylan tickets. We were about 100th in the queue, and the line snaked back into Soho and right up to Oxford Street. The box office was opening at 9:00 the next morning. It became like a carnival. First the football crowds appeared after their games had finished and gawked at us. Then the film and theater people, then the nightclubs. Along the line people ate, played music, and generally created a carnival atmosphere. By 4 a.m. things were beginning to quieten down, and some of us went off to a sauna to keep ourselves awake. The cafés opened at 6 a.m. to give us all coffee and breakfast, and with mounting excitement we waited for the 9 a.m. start. At 8:30 everyone stood up and the line began to shuffle forward. We got to the front desk pretty quickly. "Only four tickets each," they cried as we moved toward our destination. I arrived, paid, and got my tickets. When I got home I found that they had given me five tickets rather than four.

That sense of community was also present in festivals. Seeing John Martyn on a Saturday afternoon in Glastonbury in 1979. Dancing with 5,000 people to Sister Sledge singing "We Are Family," seeing Supertramp endure a power cut in the middle of their set, and encouraging everyone to sing community songs like "Roll out the Barrel."

I lived in Notting Hill Gate in London. It was then known as "the front line," one of the only places in London where you could buy drugs on the street through the huge alternative community that also lived there. During the carnival the place was transformed into one huge festival, and that sense of magically breaking through the structures of society was particularly evident.

Gradually there grew in me a sense of connection that superseded the structures of society. Punk, Bowie, the New Romantics, Patti Smith, all rolled into one. One of my favorite lines of rebellion came from "Gloria" on Patti Smith's album *Horses*: "Jesus died for somebody's sins, but not mine." It seemed to sum up the perfect way to give the middle finger to the society that had created all my pain and trouble.

That sense of magic existed in the development of the counterculture in Western society. Woodstock and its nemesis Altamont, Haight-Ashbury, Glastonbury, Camden in London, Stonehenge, Avebury, Greenham Common, The Convoy, all represented that search for connectedness, for that magic. The same magic that took the Beatles to India and saw numerous cults and self-awareness groups form over the '70s and '80s: Bhagwan Shree Rajneesh, TM, Hare Krishna, EST, all came out of that same desire to see life in a different way.

To some extent I got involved by accident. I ended up in India as a part of a trekking party to Nepal. There was no great desire to take a spiritual path. I just wanted to take a holiday. But when you are 14,000 feet up a mountain at night with a full moon illuminating a sea of clouds beneath you, and snowy peaks breaking through those clouds like icebergs your brain gets messed up. I did not think that anything had really changed. My mother said that she noticed the difference when she saw me come òff the plane wearing Indian clothes and claiming to be vegetarian.

More than anything else, that month-long trip to India sealed my fate. Up till then I had been a "part-time" hippy. I hung out where it suited me, and then returned to normal life to earn a living. I had a foot in both camps. I still traded on my background, my school, my university degree, and my ambition to get on, but spent evenings and weekends dealing with the fall-out of not fitting in by adopting an alternative lifestyle.

This changed when I came back from India. What I had previously thought of as a nice magical escape from a sense of aloneness, transformed into a clear idea that there might be another way of looking at things, and that this alternative reality was in fact truer than that which society held up as being real.

Maybe the constructs of our society—hard work, a good reputation, family life, money, pensions, careers, patriotism, political ideology, and the like—might all be social constructs founded on no more than expediency? The idea being: "What has worked for us all in the past will surely work for us all in the present, and in the future. With a few minor adjustments brought about by progress and technology."

This was set against the idea that there was a reality, hidden from view, that suggested that everything was connected. That there was a spiritual dimension that went way beyond the horizon of conventional Judeo-Christian belief; and that this reality was not just a social construct, but had its roots in the experienced wisdom of enlightened masters. That when you got "enlightened" you were able to see that reality. And once you had seen it, nothing would ever be the same again. I now embarked upon the goal of "enlightenment" full time.

The truth is that, up to this moment, I had had no real interest in this "spirituality"; but now it seemed like a way through. And by that, I mean a way through that experience of pain and aloneness. If I could find a new basis for reality that enabled me to somehow move my experience on to another plain, to include all that I was experiencing, but provide a greater context within which to hold it, then I might be able to find a sustainable way of creating a way forward.

In reality, I continued my life much the same. It was just that there was now a possibility of something changing. A hope that there might be more than I had realized up to now. I started off with Paramahansa Yogananda's *Autobiography of a Yogi* and took it from there.

I sought out courses, tried meditation, did a version of EST, and generally threw myself into the business of getting enlightened, and after six months I had the experience I was looking for.

I describe that experience in my previous book, *Developing Consciousness: A Roadmap of the Journey to Enlightenment* (and it is at the back of this book as the Appendix). The effect of it was that somehow I broke through into what I thought was a greater understanding of what was real. Looking back on it I would not say that I was enlightened, just that I had an experience that convinced me that there was more to life than what we see day to day. That there was a spiritual dimension to existence connecting everything. That I was a part of something greater than my individual consciousness, and through the experience of that greater consciousness I was linked into the essential Life-Force that was behind everything.

It is at this moment that I accepted the idea that there was that Life-Force, and that the universe really was a friendly place. It was an experience that altered the course of my life. I had seen something that was apparently not seen by most people. And thus, the way I saw reality was different from the accepted "Newtonian" view of things.

For me, there was now a connection between everything. Life was not random, rather it invited participation and cooperation. And I saw it as my duty to communicate this experience. As a result, I left the job I had in advertising and joined a self-awareness group who had the aim of promoting these ideas.

Interestingly enough, although the context of my life changed, my lifestyle remained relatively the same. I still struggled with relationships, there was still a dysfunctionality about my emotional life, and I still felt as if I were on a roller coaster, albeit with greater highs and lows, and a bigger horizon. It was almost as if I had changed the worldview that I held, but I continued the same behavior within that worldview.

Whereas before my life had been more about sex and drugs and rock and roll and advertising and parties, now it became about the evolution of consciousness, about the oneness of everything, about spirituality… and about sex and drugs and rock and roll. I was still dysfunctional within a highly functional context; and that more functional context accelerated the magical consciousness that was at the route of this trajectory.

I interpreted this new reality as giving me powers of creation. I could supposedly "intend" things to happen. I could speak things into being. Being a part of a greater consciousness gave me an "all-powerful" aspect to my normal ego consciousness. It was not that I thought I was Jesus or Napoleon. More that I could bend the normal rules of reality because I had an insight into them. They always say that there is a fine line between genius and insanity, and to some extent I trod that fine line.

The small group of six that I worked with "spoke into being" a company of over three hundred, entered politics and ran two election campaigns, one in a general election linked to a major political party, and ended up as a management consultancy based in Knightsbridge. True, there was a lot of hard work; but there was also an understanding that the world could work through magic, that by connecting to that greater source anything was possible, and that there was a short road between thinking something and making it happen. I can remember in the sales room of the marketing department we had a meditation stool, and if the sales figures did not go up, someone had to sit on that stool and stare at the sales board till it moved.

There seemed to be an understood link between intending something to happen and it actually happening, which belied the need to move the nuts and bolts of everyday reality to make that happen.

That magical reality took the idea that the universe was a friendly place and our role was to cooperate with that friendly universe to a point where we did not just cooperate, but could manipulate it as well. Somehow the ego and intention were combined in a way that ended up with reality being shifted in the direction that was intended. This also happens in concepts of prayer within the religious life. The idea that we can ask the supposed almighty God (whatever that is) to help us win a war, or a game of football, or make granny better, has a similar quality about it.

I am not saying that these prayers do not have purpose or meaning; what I am saying is that they are based on the same magical consciousness that assumes that our egotistical wants and desires can be translated into actuality through a connection with an ultimate consciousness. There is a veracity about it. However, the weakness is in the link to our personal whims and desires. For example, both sides of a conflict praying to the same God for victory.

I can remember the day that I moved on from this way of thinking. I had not been happy in the group that I worked with for some time. I had left a job in advertising working in the West End of London in order to do something a bit more idealistic: I wanted to change the world, and I assumed that the magical connection that I had with reality would help me with that. Now, fourteen years later, I was working in a marketing company in the West End of London, doing much the same sort of things that I had been doing previously: working for clients, wearing a suit, and somewhere in the back of my mind thinking that I was doing it all for the greater good.

I was on a running machine in the Hiatt Carlton Hotel off Sloane Street, and wondering whether or not I should leave this company that I had worked with for those fourteen years: through being with six people, three hundred people, in politics, in training, and in marketing. Should I leave or should I stay? Suddenly I heard a voice in my head. "Would you be prepared to die for me?" The thought came as a bit of a bolt out of the blue, but I considered it. Would I be prepared to die for my beliefs? That is how I interpreted it. In the end, I reasoned that I was a fairly arrogant sod and, if it came down to it, I would be prepared to die for my beliefs. "Well," came back the voice, "if you are prepared to die for your beliefs, what is the big deal about leaving this company?" And I thought, "what *is* the big deal?" So, I went back to the office and resigned.

Since then I have not held the same belief in that magical consciousness. I consider it, I pray for things, but I have more of a holistic perspective about the nature of prayer. It has something to do with willingness, openness, cooperation, not expecting a result but participating in the possibility of one. But there remains a sense that anything is possible, that miracles are possible, and miracles are after all a part of that magic. I like the explanation of miracles as being "events that do not conform to natural law as we currently understand it." Giving us all wiggle room to include the fact that miracles do conform to natural law, the problem is only in the scope of our understanding.

I do have a sense that being connected to a greater whole and cooperating with that greater whole might bring about unexpected results, and that I am doing something that is fundamentally right, even if I do not quite understand the nature of that rightness. All of which goes to say that you never fully lose one of these states of consciousness. You might move through them, but you come back to them as and when it suits you. They are not good or bad, one is not better than the other; they are just different ways of looking at life.

In the last year, I have taken part in a circle dance to celebrate the coming of spring, I have used rocks to denote manhood, I have gathered sticks and plants at harvest-time, I have walked a labyrinthine "Winter Garden" to simulate the coming of winter. I have celebrated the beginning of lent by putting ash on my forehead, and I have celebrated that universal word ritual of Holy Communion… all of which have magical connotations. The idea is that when you do something in one place, it has an effect in all places.

Such rituals have always played a big part in all societies, and will continue to do so.

Be Careful What You Get Involved With

1987

Social events are a very important part of community building, and so one year we decided to hold a special event on May Day.

It was going to be an all-day party with 250 people coming to a formal breakfast in a tent, with a talk on the idea of spring.

Everyone was to wear spring colors of white, green, and yellow.

All this was to take place in a country house estate, and in the middle of the huge garden we erected a maypole.

It was not enough to just dance around the maypole. We wanted to explain the meaning of the maypole as a fertility symbol, so we wrote a play.

It involved eight girls (all around twenty years old), who were all to be dressed in white, representing the "virgins" of a small mediaeval English village.

These girls went off to visit the local "crone," or wise old woman, to find out about the legendary character "John of the Green," who was supposed to appear in the woods around May Day.

The crone warned the young girls never to go to the woods around that time, otherwise their purity would be ruined, as John of the Green was supposed to attack young girls and make them pregnant.

Unbeknown to either the girls or the crone, the local lads had been secretly listening in to this conversation, and decided to ambush the girls if they came into the woods.

The girls, of course, go into the woods to find the mysterious John of the Green, only to be attacked by the young lads and chased out to the maypole in the field where they all dance around symbolizing the loss of their innocence.

On the day, we formed all 250 people into circles around the maypole. Then the characters came out and performed the play, which ended with the girls taking the central position around the maypole and dancing around it to a mediaeval band, while the other 250 people danced in four concentric circles, each circle moving in a different direction.

It was a powerful and fun ritual.

Afterward, we all then sat down and had a picnic lunch before wandering around the beautiful gardens.

I did not think much more about it. The social event had worked, everybody had a good time. The weather held and dancing around the maypole was magic.

It was only the next year when I was looking to repeat the event and went to contact the girls in the play that I found out that seven out of the eight girls were unable to take part.

They had all become pregnant.

Chapter 8
Of Gods and Monsters

Mythical Consciousness

In America, it is race. In England, it is class.

An underlying and unspoken set of values and prejudices that affect the way we behave. In England, the class system is enforced through a set of behavioral rules. The brilliance of the system is that by knowing these unspoken rules you can identify whether or not someone is in your class.

The way you speak, the way you behave, what you wear, all betray the class you come from. The way you move up the class ladder is by learning how to behave. And if you do not know how to behave, those around you will be easily able to recognize you as being of a "different" class, while you yourself are completely unaware that you have broken any codes of behavior because you did not know that these codes even existed.

It is all about giving yourself away. Calling a lavatory a "toilet" shows you up, or calling a "sitting room" a "lounge," or a "sofa" a "settee." All these expressions denote one class from another. Eating is particularly tricky. You have to learn which knife and fork to use and when. How to properly hold the knife, fork, or spoon, and how to bring the food from your plate to your mouth. Do any of these things wrongly, and you betray yourself as "not coming from the top draw."

And it works at every level. Middle-class people will recognize lower-class people by their behavior; behavior that the lower class will be completely ignorant of. Upper-middle-class people can spot middle-class people. Upper-class people can spot upper-middle-class people; and the aristocracy have their own set of rules. Only the queen is impervious. Everyone else is subject to these rules and made to feel inadequate by the class above them. Right up to the monarch. And she feels the obligation to keep it all going for everyone else.

It is all about "not letting the side down." In other words, making sure that you behave correctly so that the class you belong to can be seen to be upholding the standards that your friends and family have aspired to over all the previous years. It is known as "Good Form," or "Bad Form." Good form is doing what is expected of you. Bad form is breaking the rules of your class. It is very bad form not to pay your gambling debts. It is also bad form to wear the wrong clothes at Royal Ascot. It is bad form to drink your soup out of the front of a soup spoon, and good form to drink it out of the side. It is bad form for a union man to break a picket line. It is good form to serve your country. It is bad form to wear brown shoes with a blue suit, good form to wear black.

Bad form to pass the port the wrong way at dinner. Good form to write a thank-you note to your hostess. Bad form to call a woman of age by her first name when you meet for the first time. Good form to stand up if you are sitting when a woman comes into a room. Good form to be able to send your children to private school. Bad form not to, if you can afford it.

Many people will tell you that these rules do not apply any more, that it is all about money, that we are becoming more classless. But don't believe a word of it. These are rules hidden in plain sight, and only those "in the know" are aware. Some may get relaxed, but others will take their place.

You can have all the money in the world, but your status can be immediately undermined by someone whispering to a confidant, "New money!"

The class system is designed to keep everyone in their place so that those above can feel superior to those below, and those below have something to aspire to. All classes collude in maintaining the system. Meritocracy might be in fashion, but fashion is only transient, and the value system recognizes that. You can see it most clearly in the House of Lords. Those serving used to do so by way of inheriting a title from their family. However, there are also now "Life Peers," people who are made Lords for life because of political allegiance or achievement. They are known by the hereditary Lords as "Day Boys." A reference to the lower status of people who go to boarding schools, but opt to go home to their parents in the evening.

I entered this system at the middle to upper level: I came from a "good family," which means it had a history written down in books that list such families (*Debrett's Peerage*), I went to private schools, my father served as an officer in the army (generally officers were seen as being a higher class than the "other ranks"). My grandfather had been knighted for being in the army, and we all knew how to hold our knives and forks the "right way." (Second finger of the left hand over the arch of the fork, handle of the fork under the palm of that hand. Knife held with first finger over the place where the blade meets the handle, thumb to the side, handle nestled under the palm, never over the top like a pencil!)

But not having a father put us at a disadvantage. We were to some extent a "charity job," always after scholarships and at the behest of the generosity of others (good form to accept, bad form to expect!).

All this good form and bad form was particularly pronounced in the 1950s and 1960s, when I grew up, because of the war. This caused much loss and heartache, which the church was unable to cope with because it had lost so much authority. All there was to rely on was whether you behaved well or not. The church had always been on the higher end of the class systems. It was said that the very act of joining a church moved you from being lower class to lower-middle class, because you began to associate with the different people that went to church.

Also, during both world wars the church threw its lot in with the ruling class and encouraged everyone to fight for "God and Country." The resultant carnage left the church with more than egg on its face, and many people swore never to trust it again. Consequently, church attendance fell off a cliff after the Second World War and has never recovered. So, what was there left to trust in?

Well, good form, of course. It was good form to fight, bad form to run away, good form to suffer in silence, bad form to complain. Good form to have a stiff upper lip (not be subject to your emotions), bad form to blubber on (cry).

The generation that began to have kids in the 1950s was so emotionally scarred by two world wars, and all the austerity that went with it, that how you behaved became even more important, which is why the '60s came as such a shock.

This all relates to a "mythical consciousness" in that this is the stage where morality rules. Like in all the great mythical stories there are gods, and if you behave well the gods will reward you; if not, there will be punishment. The use of carrot and stick is the basis of mythical consciousness.

The punishment for behaving badly in society was ostracization from your class, the equivalent of excommunication from the church, which was again all about a mythical consciousness. Before the Second World War, divorce would subject a woman to ostracization (read W. Somerset Maugham), imprison a man, and so on. It was a heavy punishment, because none of your friends would talk to you, for fear that they too would be ostracized by association. Look at Oscar Wilde.

I was born into this system, and was eventually sent away to school (good form), where I was miserable and did not do well (not good form, but not quite bad form). And there were more gods. Other pupils and masters all with expected behavior codes. Not quite on a class level, but still with a high degree of reward and punishment. These gods had to be appeased in order for me to live a quiet life. Cross them and the result was both physical and emotional violence.

The first time I ever felt safe at school was at an off-site Bible meeting with the local vicar. We were driven to the vicarage for religious instruction, and although I cannot quite remember the details (I must have been ten or eleven), I got a distinct feeling that this was a place of safety. That no one was going to attack me, that the master (vicar) was benign, and that what was being spoken about offered some kind of safety. It was a very comforting feeling, and it resulted in me joining the school choir. Here I found a place that I could do well. I had a good voice and rose through the ranks to become head chorister. At my next school, this rather turned against me because my voice broke very late and to my chagrin, I ended up winning the "Unbroken Voice Singing Competition" at the age of sixteen. Having the award presented to me at speech day was a source of great humiliation rather than pride.

But something stuck from that first Bible study. It was not that I was religious. I do not think I wrestled with whether I "believed" or not, more that I found a new set of rules that seemed to offer more security than I had been offered before. Being in the choir was just a part of that, and when I was confirmed at the age of sixteen it was really a case of joining that particular club. I had visions of divine intervention at the moment of confirmation by the bishop, but nothing happened and I was grateful for the presents that came as a result. This was just the swapping of one god for another. I paid my dues and joined in. The rules and the consequences around how one behaved, at that time, were very strong.

I think one of the reasons I did not run away from my first boarding school was that somehow I knew it was bad form. And the reason I was not able to tell my mother was that it would have been bad form to pass on my suffering to her. I was not an eager recruit to any of these clubs and societies that defined the rules that steered my life. I just accepted them and got on with it.

To begin with my mother ruled (or tried to), then the schools and various pupil cultures had their codes of behavior. The school banned such things as touching other people's property (stealing) or fraternizing after lights out (talking or touching). It defined how to behave when coming across a teacher in a quad (index finger raised to the chest as a salute), demonstrated how to play games without excessive violence (unless the school pride was at stake), and suggested the need to do well at exams.

For pupils the rules were obvious: No grassing up, house and school before self, and all the various "good forms" that had been instilled in us by our parents. Anyone referring to the lavatory as a "toilet" was subject to merciless bullying (see Sebastian Faulks's book, *Engleby*, for more of this; I went to school with Faulks).

I just about got by. I did not do much work, until that is I was informed by my tutor at the age of fifteen that he expected me to fail all my exams. This had an electric effect. Not because I wanted to do well and please him, but because I thought, "Sod you, I am going to prove you wrong." Like so much rebellion, you are still operating from within the system by opposing it. The very act of opposition reinforces the status quo, because it comes from the same self-interested worldview. There is a lovely quote from Einstein: "No problem can be solved from the same level of consciousness that created it." My decision to work did not involve a shift in consciousness; it was simply my method of resistance.

And I worked: I passed my exams and I went to university. But it was still all about "appeasing the gods." It was not inspired, or visionary, it was a way of surviving those gods. In fact, they had such a hold over me that when it was suggested that I go and work on an Australian sheep station for a year "to toughen me up" I jumped at the chance. As if I needed toughening up after ten years of boarding school. But, once again I appeased those gods, bought into their way of thinking.

In Australia there was also a "code of behavior" that I had to follow. It was muscular, brutal, and ended with a clichéd attempt by the other sheep hands (or Jackeroos as they were known, girls were Jillaroos) to cut off all my hair in the sheering sheds. I fought them off, won respect, and the wheel turned yet again. More rules, more gods, more behavior that I fell into.

Arriving at Bristol University was the first time I began to feel the hold of those codes of behavior begin to relax. The community was more mixed, and not much was expected of you. There were not that many codes to observe, except wearing jeans, smoking, and getting up at midday. You did not even have to go to lectures or work. I opted to study economic and social history, not because I was really interested in it, but I had got good results in my school exams, and there seemed to be fewer facts you had to remember and much that you could make up.

I drifted through life at Bristol and split my time between working in broadcasting at the local radio station and hanging out with friends. To some extent I bought my friends. Coming from an upper-middle-class family with no father I had been left money by an aunt, and therefore had enough to buy a house. This I did, and then invited friends to come and live with me at a cheap rent. Three of them said yes, and interestingly enough we are still friends to this day. Whether or not that would have happened without me buying the house is another matter.

By now any involvement in religion was a distant memory. I did not once enter a church from the age of nineteen, when I left school, till the age of forty, apart from the odd wedding, funeral, and Christmases with the parent (good form). I drifted into advertising, and throughout that time, apart from the need to work and be with friends, the idea of gods and morality troubled me little.

It was when I came back from India and left advertising that I reentered that realm of morality. Spirituality is not by itself moral. Archbishop Rowan Williams's definition of spirituality is "The cultivation of a sensitive and rewarding relationship with eternal truth and love." And to me that is not about right and wrong, or codes of behavior, or appeasing one god or another, but is more about growing relationships, with the essence of eternal truth and love (however you define that). But spiritual communities? That's another thing. Just as there is a thin line between insanity and genius, so there is a thin line between spiritual community and cult. Where does one end and the other begin?

And, once again, I was drawn into a new set of behaviors. Not this time in terms of good form and bad form (although it is good form to join a spiritual community and bad form to join a cult), but in terms of "what works" to serve the aims of the spiritual community. I joined a group that was putting on self-awareness seminars. That went on to form a marketing company using people who had been through the seminars as staff. We then went into politics and ended up as a marketing consultancy. But within that we had highly organized codes of behavior, we had lectures on subjects such as "The earth as an organism," and being a part of that group took so much time and effort that we often left behind our friends and our families. Serving the purpose of the "transformation of society" was everything. And to that end we would do anything.

We came in at 8:00, had a morning meeting every day with all the staff, worked through till often past 7, and every Friday had an end of the week meeting with the whole company. The group was controversial and appeared in national television "exposés" three times. We often had weekend meetings, once danced together naked wearing only animal masks, chartered two planes and took everyone (three hundred people) on holiday to Egypt for three weeks, did the same for less people to Turkey (twice), Morocco, Tahiti, and Ibiza.

There was a leadership that decided on correct behavior, and once again if you went outside those codes, then you often lost membership. There was definitely a "good" way of behaving and a "bad way," mostly about how much effort you put in, your level of commitment, and your willingness to do whatever was necessary to get the result. If you conformed, you advanced; if you did not conform, you did not survive. It was a curious mixture of Christmas parties at the Dorchester, week-long fasts, community meetings, meditation, and always work, work, and more work.

We would try every management fad. We went in for "Creative Aggression" (a therapy developed in American prisons where two people shouted the worst at each other and hit each other with foam rubber sticks to "clear" relationships), Neuro Linguistic Programming, Finger Counting, Goal Setting, Outward Bound trips, and any number of other ways to try to do better.

In mythical consciousness, you tend to give up personal "will" to the will of the god that is worshipped, and that god sets the behavioral codes based upon the given morality. To that extent this level of consciousness lets go of its own will and settles for whatever is offered by the god.

This is not really giving up to a Life-Force, as it is much more giving up to an idea of what a Life-Force might be. It is an idealized fabricated reality that you exist within. The god in question might be a parent, a country, a religion, a leader, or a culture, and as such it is a "made-up" thing rather than the essence of all life. There is a letting go into this morality, but also a drive toward whatever perceived good is offered.

After fourteen years I left that group, mainly because I had strayed too far from the original purpose I had, which was to communicate my experience of the nature of reality. I had ended up working in a marketing company, albeit a slightly strange one. There was only one direction I could see myself going next, and that was toward the church.

Up till that point, I had always seen the church as the "bag lady" of spirituality, like one of those women who walk around the streets with a supermarket trolley filled with items that are seemingly useless, but precious to them. The church had all that useless baggage, but the one thing going for it was that you could talk about God and not be considered mad. I thought of becoming a Buddhist or a Hindu, but I have had my "colors" done, and yellow just isn't my color. Also, I did not fancy changing my name to Prem Anand Something-or-other, quite apart from the fact that my mother would never have forgiven me.

Communicating this change to my mother was difficult. Leaving advertising and joining a weird self-awareness group had not gone down well, definitely bad form. I tried to break it gently. I began by telling my mother I had been to church the other day. "Very nice dear," she commented. Then, a month later, I mentioned I had met the bishop. "How interesting." Finally, I let it be known that I was thinking of being ordained. The penny finally dropped and a look of horror came over her face. "Ordained!" she said, "Couldn't you just be a lay reader?"

The idea had not gone down well; however, it seems that her friends had different ideas. When she told them of my plans, they said, "The church? How marvelous, dear! What a good idea!" It seems that going into the church was, in fact, good form, and therefore something to be approved of and celebrated. The following week she sent me a Bible verse for the first time ever. "How beautiful on the mountains are the feet of those who bring good news," Isaiah 52:7. We are now the best of friends.

I was, in fact, exchanging one god for another, as the church has its own unique morality: good behavior and bad behavior; rewards and punishments. Although it is supposed to be all about that Life-Force, so much of Christian doctrine is about oughts and shoulds. Mainly because once it became an established religion with the Emperor Constantine in AD 300 it was used as a way of controlling people. And, since then, the church has had to use fear and guilt to keep people in line.

I fell into the established behavior codes quite easily. They kept me clean, and I found that they did not hinder what I wanted to do. It was almost as if, after all the years, I was able to live with these gods, and not be subject to their morality. I was no longer serving the god in order to get the reward. Nor was I keeping the morality in order to avoid being punished. Something greater was beginning to come through.

Saved by Ermine and Pearls

1994

I was now unemployed, and my goal was to be ordained in the church.

I was living in the Fulham Palace Road, in London, and cycled down to the nearest church to join.

It was a "Church of England" church, and I had form in that denomination: I had been in the school choir, I had been baptized, I had been confirmed, and although I not been to church for twenty years, I had read plenty of books and could speak the lingo.

I met up with the local parish priest. "Hi! My name is Nicholas Vesey and I would like to be ordained."

I joined.

To begin with I was given the parish magazine to edit, something to do with my advertising background.

I did my research and found the most modern church in the local area and went looking for how they did their magazine.

I turned up at the church door to be met by a receptionist. "Oh," she said, "you'll want to speak to the communications director!"

The fact that a church had both a receptionist and a communications director was pretty unique in my book, and as it turned out this was one of the first Evangelical mega-churches in the UK.

I was given a tour of the building: All hi-tech with television monitors, the latest sound system, and impossibly attractive young people all off to "Bible study."

I was sold. It was the best fun you could have in church with your clothes on: They ate and drank, had a fantastic social life, and generally created a scene that you wanted to be a part of.

The only problem was that I was not quite "kosher." They knew it and I knew it, but no one said anything. I was just not buying the Jesus being the only way to God bit, the antigay stuff, the demonic effects of yoga, or the Bible being the literal word of God.

Still it was fun and the people were great.

I was at a drinks party (there were many) at the Central Methodist Hall in Westminster one night when I spotted this extraordinary-looking woman dressed in ermine and pearls. We began chatting.

"Oh, I'm planning on being ordained," I told her grandly. She nodded thoughtfully.

"And have you accepted Jesus Christ as your Lord and Savior?" she asked me casually.

I thought about it. "No, actually I haven't," I replied.

Kindly, she then gave me more space than the Sahara Desert to consider my position, before moving off to talk to someone else.

And there was the rub. I was planning to be ordained, and yet I was not really "in the club."

The problem was that I did not really go for all the hell and damnation bit, so the idea of a unique salvation didn't chime too readily either.

All the PR around the Church of England was that it was basically barmy, but well meaning. It believed a lot of things that went out with the inquisition, and yet it looked after those who fell through the net. It was also permissible to talk about God. If anyone else talked about God they were deeply suspicious. When you said you were a Church of England priest, they invited you in for tea.

I decided to confront the problem head on. I had a good meditation practice that had been going for about five years, and so the next day I decided to test it out. The whole Jesus coming into your life thing.

I sat down and basically did one of those "is there anyone out there?" prayers, and then followed it with "If there is, could you come and make yourself known?"

Well, the amazing thing was that something did happen.

It is a bit like when you install a new app on your phone, an icon appears to tell you it is there.

There was a new icon on my consciousness, and I felt its presence.

My first experience was one of shame. I realized that in all the time I had been concerned with my own spiritual life I had never really served anyone but myself. It had all been about me: How I felt, how I wanted to be enlightened. I had not even considered others.

As I sat with that, I then had a second experience, and that was one of joy. The joy that I was no longer alone. That there was some presence that was now with me.

And then I realized that I was now "kosher." That I had joined the club. That somehow, I had jumped through those hoops that the woman in ermine and pearls had spoken about.

I did not become a card-carrying, Bible-believing fundamentalist, but a veil was drawn aside; and what it revealed was the depth of the Christian tradition.

Not just the public face, but the contemplative depth of the Desert Fathers, the mystical tradition of both Meister Eckhart and Therese of Avila. The deep darkness of John of the Cross, the optimism of Julian of Norwich, and the sanity of some contemporary theologians.

There was a sacred understanding that made Christianity just as much an "Eastern religion" as Buddhism or Hinduism or Taoism.

The concept of enlightened truth was there in the depths of it all, and this freed me from that choking morality of that mythical consciousness.

I realized I was home.

Chapter 9
Cunning Plans

Rational Consciousness

I think of myself as pretty rational. Most of us do. Rational, from the Latin word *ratio*, meaning "reckoning, numbering, calculation." We tend to work out what the best thing to do is, and then do it. Our lives are a summation of all the good ideas we have been able to put into practice; and yet the road to hell is said to be paved with good intentions, and all of us end up in some sort of trouble, no matter how rational we have been about the decisions we have made.

Because it is not just about being rational, it is also about what we are trying to achieve by being rational. It is not simply one good thought after another, it is one good thought after another toward a specific end.

The breakthrough in scientific thought came when we stopped trying to prove that the earth was the center of the universe because it said so in the Bible, and started trying to work out what was really going on for the sake of the science itself. That led to Galileo being thrown into prison because he dared to challenge the church, and also gave rise to the birth of evidence-based theory that ushered in "the enlightenment." Before that, the purpose of rational thought was to find out what was happening within the truth given by the Bible. Subsequently, it became about science for science sake. This new purpose redefined the context for rational thought.

Rational thought was now about what works, within a given context. How do we get light from electricity? How can we produce food cheaper? There is a goal, or a purpose, and we use reason to work out how.

In our own lives we have all had different circumstances, perspectives, and purposes, and we have used our rational minds to bring about the ends we have sought.

Before the age of nine, I experienced myself in a family that was just about coping with living from day to day. Financially we were sort of OK, but emotionally we were all at sea. My ultimate aim in life was to feel connected in a way that our family was not, and so my rational approach to life was to do things that made me feel connected. And that was generally served by getting my mother's attention, hence me "acting up" most of the time. When I was sent away to school I had a whole new set of circumstances.

To begin with I still felt alone and disconnected, and used the same rationale that I had used at home, namely acting up to get attention. I very quickly learned that this simply produced a shit load of trouble, both from the masters who found me impossible to deal with, and the other boys who saw me as sport.

So as not to influence others, my desk was put against the front wall of the classroom, next to the blackboard. That way the teacher felt I was not in a position to cause trouble. At break time, fights broke out. Someone stuck a ballpoint in my arm, so I stuck them with a pencil. Very quickly I learned that my aim was not to be connected, but to survive.

I adjusted my rationale accordingly. My thinking was all about how to keep out of trouble. That led to my decision to disengage emotionally, a very rational decision based on my overall aim of survival. It was only when I decided that my overall aim was to pass my exams that I once again shifted my behavior. Rationally I saw that working hard was the way to achieve what I wanted, so I threw myself into study. My overall aim had changed, and so had my mindset.

Once I had passed my exams I began to develop this idea that I wanted to "get on." Where, I did not know. I had no real desire to do anything, other than to meet someone to love and have the family I never had when growing up. But that is not a proper career, so it did not count. I rationalized that it would "do me good" to go to Australia and work on a sheep station. Then I thought that three years at college would give me enough time to work out what I really wanted to do.

At college, my overall aim became finding friends. I was not desperate to do well in my course, as I only saw it as a stop gap between school and something else. I wanted to connect with people so as to feel a sense of community. Community has always been a key rationale in my life, presumably to compensate for what I saw as a lack of love. I created community at university, in the group that I was a part of for fourteen years, and, of course, church life is all about community.

This was the first time I saw creating community as an aim I had in life, and so made that community with my friends and the house we lived in. But I noticed that I wanted more. It was as if, in all my life, I had never really been noticed. I was always skulking around somewhere as the person least likely to succeed at anything. Not good at sports, not good with women, not good intellectually, not good at making friends. The "not good at" list was pretty long. And so, I gradually developed this idea of an aim of being noticed.

One day, driving down Whiteladies Road in Bristol I saw a sign saying "BBC." It was the regional headquarters of the British Broadcasting Corporation, as well as the home of the local radio station BBC Radio Bristol. This was it—broadcasting, a way to get noticed. I just drove into the car park of the station, walked into reception, and asked if there was any way I could get a job there. The receptionist looked rather puzzled and asked me who I was. I said I was a student, and she pointed down the corridor and said, "Third door on the right." It turns out there was a student program on the station and I was in.

Over the next couple of years, I ended up working at the station, both on the student program, and for money as a station assistant. It fitted with my aim in life. I got noticed, and I got my voice heard. It felt good. However, I was not that good at it, especially on air. The technology was very complicated to operate, and I was always nervous. I did quite well coming up with ideas, and managed to get those ideas on both television and radio. But when I compared myself with the others on the station who all seemed so at ease "on air," I reasoned that I was not as good as them, and that therefore this was not a good career for me.

Time was going on and I needed to think about what I was going to do with my life. In terms of my motivation for a career, it was never about the money. I had been left money and that had paid for the house we lived in and also gave me a sufficient cushion not to be motivated by the need to earn money. Broadcasting fitted with my need to be heard and noticed, but I did not think I was good enough at it. One of my friends, however, had a father in advertising. And this seemed to be the next best thing. So, I applied to their graduate trainee program, and got in on the bottom level.

I organized a flat share in South Kensington, and began working at Masius Wynne Williams as an account manager. That really meant meeting with clients, briefing the creative team about ads, and then presenting what the creative team came up with back to the clients. I wore a suit and was seen as a part of the responsible side of the advertising agency. The irresponsible side of the agency came in at 10:30 a.m., wearing jeans, and left at 4 in the afternoon. They were the creative department, and I pretty instantly knew that this is where I wanted to be. It was the same rationale about being heard, but coupled with that, the work generated a lot of attention—in newspapers, on TV, in the industry. Your work became your signature.

So, I moved over to the creative department at another agency. But I soon found out there were better agencies, and by then I had developed an aim to be the best in this area. I therefore moved agencies after a year and ended up at Saatchi and Saatchi, which was seen as one of the best. My aim in life at this point was to be noticed, praised for my work, and seen as the best. With that came a "rush" of being part of a team that wanted the same thing and was willing to praise you to the heights if you delivered.

India put a stop to all that.

When I came back my life had completely changed. I wanted to "get enlightened," and as a result all the rationale about being great in advertising went out of the window. I resigned from the agency and took up a job delivering leaflets for a wine company. This looked mad, but rationally it made sense to me. My life was not going to be about selling soap powder, it was going to be about communicating the values and experiences that I had been given. All my friends and family tried to dissuade me. And when I joined the "self-awareness" group I lost all credibility in the eyes of the people I knew. I had given up a good job to join a cult.

But to me it was different; it was just the rational thing to do, based upon my goal in life. It made sense to do the trainings, even though they were highly controversial as they involved working with people in a room for three days from 9 a.m. till often passed 2 a.m. the following day, with only one break for food. It made sense when we formed a marketing company and employed three hundred people, who had all been through the self-awareness trainings, as staff. It made sense when we went into politics, for me to become a Parliamentary candidate, and to fight a couple of elections with the Social Democrat Party of the UK. All of it seemed to fit in with the rationale we had of wanting to transform society. Hopelessly idealistic, but highly motivational, it kept me going there for fourteen years. I was still dealing with a dysfunctional love life, but that took second fiddle to all the rest.

It was only when things slowed down into a marketing company that I began to reassess my situation. By now I had been through most of the money I had been left, but I still found that money was not a motivation. When I left the company I was unemployed, renting a room in someone else's house, and on benefits.

The church was the rational next step. If I wanted to talk about the "God bit," that was the only place to be. I was accepted into theological college, and while waiting a year took another job. For the first time, it was for money. I worked for a year as a creative director in a secretarial recruitment company. It paid the rent and put food on the table. My aim was to get to seminary, and I needed money to live before then.

At the seminary, my aim was to get ordained and to find a job in a church. As a result, I did well. I passed my exams and became president of the student body. I also made a decision that I would stop looking for a way of fulfilling my need to find a wife. This had always been my Achilles' heel. All through my career I had continued to struggle with it. My desire to "get on" with my aims in life had been primary, but underneath I still had that need for love. At college, I decided to put it to one side and rationalized that if it was meant to be, then it was meant to be, but I was not going to try for it any more.

I was ordained into the Church of England in Rochester Cathedral in June 1997. From there I took a job as an assistant priest in a parish in Tunbridge Wells, Kent. I was now in a different paradigm. My aim in life was still to communicate the values I had held to since India, and now I had a platform from which to speak.

I threw myself into working in the church. It seemed rational to engage in local community building as that was so much a part of a vision of life that integrated the spiritual with the commonplace. I organized events and worked at bringing the communities together. I also met my wife.

She was twenty years younger than me, and having made a decision not to get involved in more of the same, I steered clear of her to begin with. One Sunday she phoned me up at 10 p.m. to ask me "how I was getting on." I took that as a clear signal of intent from her part. Three years later we were married in the church where I was assistant priest.

Although my life was then very much about communicating spiritual values, it is also clear to me that some of the underlying issues that I had been facing all my life were being resolved. Not only did I get married, but I was also involved in a great deal of community building, all of which went some way to healing my emotional disquiet. And although I did not rationally think it through, it seems to me that somewhere deep down I was resolving things without consciously thinking them through.

After five years we moved to Norwich where I became a vicar, a priest in charge of a parish. Here my aim was to develop some of the ideas I had been thinking through while training and at my first parish. I wrote a course, and from that I wrote my first book: *Developing Consciousness: A Roadmap of the Journey to Enlightenment.*

We created an alternative community within the church, using drumming and "folk religion" to explore some of the basic ideas of modern spirituality. This meant reinterpreting Christianity as an "Eastern religion," and using the contemplative tradition of Christianity to make links with other established religions. We also had children. Samuel was born in 2004 and Jessica in 2006. I had arrived at a point where life seemed to have come together and I was living the rational extension of the values and aims that I had set myself to live by.

As far as length of time working in one church goes, three years is seen as too short a time, seven years is seen as just right, fourteen years is seen as lucky, twenty-one years as too long. I had been in Norwich for fourteen years when my wife, Heather, and I decided to go to a hotel to think about "what next?"

Over a conversation I casually asked her what she wanted. "How about something 'airy,'" she replied. We had been to America before. I had written my first book over a couple of months in Albuquerque, so I said, "How about America?" I logged on to the American Episcopal website. And there, third on the list was the Aspen Chapel. I had heard of Aspen, so I clicked on the link. Two phone calls and one Skype interview later we were on the plane to Aspen for an interview. This would represent another change in my purpose in life, and therefore created a new rationale.

Up till that time my role was focused on the Church of England. However, over the twenty years I had worked in the church I began to see the nature of the relationship between the church and the state as something that hindered its spiritual message. In some ways, the purpose of the church was to give credibility to the monarchy and the state.

The church crowned the monarch and validated the state by bishops being a part of the House of Lords. At every level, the church's job was to give credibility to the state. You even swore an oath of allegiance to the monarchy at ordination. There was also a collusion at times of war, when it was very difficult for the church to speak out against a war because of the national interest. In fact, the church had lost much of its authority due to its support of conscription during both world wars. As a result, the Christian story had to be told in a certain way so that church and state could be seen to be as one, because one fed power to the other. Jesus was born of a virgin, died for our sins on the cross, and the Bible, or at least the New Testament, was to be swallowed whole. This was the church view, and the state view, and the two went together—in liturgy, in prayers, in Parliament, and with the monarch. Any other interpretation was merely fringe, and therefore not the real thing.

I found these attitudes increasingly difficult, and the idea of going to America opened up a new way of approaching religion and spirituality. Despite being on the Episcopal website, the Aspen Chapel was not an Episcopal church, it was nondenominational: Although it was rooted in the Christian religion, belief in one thing or another was not important. The purpose of the church was to explore how to "live life more skillfully," irrespective of what you believed, and so all the basic wisdom traditions in the major religions became a part of the tools one could use to explore the possibilities of spiritual development. I would therefore be able to broaden my aim to be one that included all these traditions, as well as the one I was ordained into.

We spent a week in Aspen considering what life would be like there. When we were offered the job, my wife and I gave both the children (then aged eight and ten) a veto. We would all decide to go, or not at all.

Taking the Plunge
1996

It is a big step deciding to be ordained. Actually, one is not supposed to decide for oneself. In the Church of England your community suggests it to you and you say, "Who me?"

And then there is what is known as a "process of discernment," where you meet the archdeacon, then the bishop, then a special conference that lasts two days. And after all that they tell you if they think you are "suitable to go forward."

After you have been chosen you have to decide which seminary to go to.

I ended up in Durham at St. John's College.

I arrived there at the age of forty, only to discover I was back at university again. I was in a single room of a hall of residence, there was a fresher's fair (dramsoc or rowing?) and I ended up spending leisurely afternoons drinking coffee in cafés, and in the evening drinking cheap booze in the students' bar. Heaven!

I even tried acting, taking the role of Lord Capulet in a college production of Romeo and Juliet.

I was fulfilling all the unfulfilled days of school. I was popular, I became head boy, I had a great time.

As a part of the course you had to go on a placement to another Anglican parish. Most people went to Guildford or Manchester, or some such local place.

I had always bought my incense from Kyoto in Japan, and fancied a visit.

I wrote to the bishop there and got an official invitation, which is how I came to spend two months looking at Buddhist meditation temples.

I also visited the factory where they made my incense. It is made very much like spaghetti, coming out wet in long thin lines. There is no stick in Japanese incense, and you do not smell it, you "listen" to it.

I went on a conference with the diocese while I was there. We all stayed in a hotel, and when I was shown to my room there were twelve other people sleeping there. It was a Japanese hotel; smart, and with all the mod cons you would expect of a Hilton. But with your futon on the floor alongside others.

They banqueted in six courses, drank all evening, sang karaoke until 3 in the morning (I went to bed at 12), and then were all up for Holy Communion at 7 and a breakfast of miso soup. It was exhausting.

Before ordination you go on a retreat with your diocesan group. Three days away at a conference facility with twenty others to get used to the idea of becoming a priest.

There are lectures, prayers, time for reflection, and communal meals.

At the end of it all you get in your car and go straight to the cathedral for the service. That is the first day you wear your clerical collar.

It is odd to see yourself in a clerical collar. It seems to change who you are. And it changes who people think you are. Wandering around town you get different looks. Some people turn away, others smile at you for no reason. There seems to be an expectation of who you are and how you will behave.

That day there was a quiet mood at breakfast, everyone in their thoughts of the day to come.

We all went out to our cars to drive the forty miles to Rochester Cathedral.

By the time I came to my car everyone had left. I got in and turned the key. The engine gasped, but would not start. Again, and the same thing happened. A panic began at the seat of my stomach and began to rise through my body. I had an hour to get there including a forty-minute drive.

I rushed into the house, but no one was there.

They only ordain once a year—the cathedral, the bishop, the choir, it is a huge event—and I was going to miss it.

One last attempt at the car. She started and I got there just in time.

Chapter 10
Chariots of Fire

Visionary Consciousness

There is more willfulness in rational consciousness than there is Life-Force. By its very nature rational consciousness involves a process of working out the best way to get to a specific end. The move to visionary consciousness is, however, almost a rational decision to let go into the Life-Force. A moment when the dreaming becomes more attractive than the reality, and new possibilities occur. Einstein is supposed to have said, "I didn't arrive at my understanding of the fundamental laws of the universe through my rational mind." And there does seem to be a moment where preparation within rational consciousness leads to a leap into something new.

I was too busy surviving to be visionary about anything. I dreamed of a wife and family, but apart from that it was all about getting by. Working in broadcasting I had a hint of the possibility of creating awareness around issues of poverty, but it was only fleeting. There was nothing of that in advertising. My trip to India and the subsequent realizations opened me up to the possibility that there might be more to life than meets the eye. I began to think that the nature of transformation might include a spiritual dimension that augmented the nuts and bolts of everyday life.

The idea of miracles being "events that do not conform to natural law as we currently understand it" opened up a world of possibilities that I found hugely attractive. I left advertising and joined the self-awareness training group because of a desire to spread these ideas. It seemed to me that I was living in a world that was hemmed in by a materialistic view, when in fact there was a whole other dimension that people were unaware of, and I felt it was my duty to communicate that idea; and those self-awareness trainings were effective. People came in wanting to get enlightened, or turn their lives around, and over three days it happened. We deconstructed the worldview that the participants held. Pointing out the inconsistences in their thinking, their lack of willingness to follow through (keeping going till 2:30 a.m. forced you to follow through), and confronting fears.

The training was highly experiential. I describe going through one in my last book, *Developing Consciousness*. They involved experiencing fear, grief, anger—whatever was there—and facing whatever was driving you in your life.

After the first two days the participants were left with a sense of wondering what could replace those thoughts and feelings, and at that point they were introduced to ideas and concepts pointing to a greater consciousness than they had previously experienced, one that was wider, more expanded. Beyond the tyranny of the mind, but highly rational when combined with a new experienced reality.

These trainings left people empowered and highly motivated to share the experience with others and with that came a vision of a society based around a shared consciousness. Most of us had a rudimentary understanding of the existence of "unitive consciousness," one that all sentient beings shared. And the idea was that this unitive consciousness was the key to understanding how to deal with the problems of the world.

If that unitive consciousness existed, then we were all equal within that consciousness. And if we were all equal, then resources and opportunities could be made available to everyone, because deep down creativity was not in the hands of the few, but in the hands of all. It was a perspective that acknowledged the Life-Force as the creator and organizer of all things, and downplayed the idea that society should force life in one direction or another.

In this paradigm, everyone was connected to that Life-Force, and all we had to do was give up to the creativity of that Life-Force, and work hard, and with that came a vision of society transformed into a fairer and more caring place.

This inspiration led to the group forming a marketing company to get enough money together to go into politics. Outwardly we were specializing in business training and marketing, working with companies to sell whatever they wanted to sell. But within the community there was an understanding that something much deeper was going on, that this was all part of an effort to shift the way society worked. It was hugely idealistic, and at its height there were over three hundred of us working there. The move into politics was driven by the same desire.

We fought a general election seat in 1987 for the British Liberal Democrats. One of us was the candidate, and we bussed hundreds of staff up to the seat to canvass on a voluntary basis. We all saw this as a possible way of communicating our enthusiasm and ideas through the medium of politics. In the end we did well, but did not win. However, the group carried on, opening offices in France and Italy.

After ten years some of the enthusiasm had waned, and we settled down into becoming a marketing consultancy. Ideas of transforming society were dropped as being unrealistic, and it really became about keeping the business alive and making money. I took that vision of transforming society into the church.

To me the Church of England was like the nation's Christmas tree, except all the lights were not working. My vision was that if one could haul the church into the twenty-first century, and have those Christmas lights come on, that would enable a more equal and fair society to come through the spiritual message of the church. Once again this was highly idealistic, but when you are wanting to make something happen it is not the rational that drives you but the visionary.

My vision was really summed up in Blake's poem "Jerusalem":

> And did those feet in ancient time,
> Walk upon England's mountains green:
> And was the holy Lamb of God,
> On England's pleasant pastures seen!
>
> And did the Countenance Divine,
> Shine forth upon our clouded hills?
> And was Jerusalem builded here,
> Among these dark Satanic Mills?
>
> Bring me my Bow of burning gold;
> Bring me my Arrows of desire:
> Bring me my Spear: O clouds unfold!
> Bring me my Chariot of fire!
>
> I will not cease from Mental Fight,
> Nor shall my Sword sleep in my hand:
> Till we have built Jerusalem,
> In England's green & pleasant Land.[1]

More than anything else this really spoke to the vision that has driven me in my life and continues to do so today. It encapsulates the thought of transformation, and all that goes into making it happen. Many people when they read that first verse just want to say no, Jesus did not visit England. But that is not what is being said here. Blake is really talking about that fundamental unitive consciousness behind all things. He is saying, is there really a part of us that is divine? Do we have access to that universal consciousness? And can it be a part of who we are here in the world?

He is making the same point that Aldous Huxley made in his Perennial Philosophy. It is a statement of the spiritual underpinning of all things. And it is the beginning of the spiritual journey. "Is the universe a friendly place?" as Einstein asked. If the answer to that is yes, then that changes everything. It means we are not alone in our quest, and we are a part of something much greater than ourselves.

In the second verse, he asks about the human realization of this divine presence. If there is such a presence, are we aware of it? Did the countenance divide? Was there an understanding that we are not alone, and if so does this enable us to found that city of Jerusalem?

Jerusalem, the symbol of a holy city, a visionary place of justice and fairness for all: could that be built here among all the chaos of human existence? And, of course, we want to say yes to that. It is an invitation to participate in the evolution of consciousness by acknowledging the existence of holiness in the present time.

The third verse is a call to arms: Arm me for this fight to bring a fairer society. Arm me with desire, with precious thoughts, with understanding, and with the wherewithal to do it. It almost has the flavor of a superhero "origins" story: Thor or Iron Man receiving their superpowers for the first time. It is calling on the Life-Force to give us everything we need to do the job. It is the rational and the visionary coming together to fulfill the potential of humanity.

And then that final verse.

> I will not cease from Mental Fight,
> Nor shall my Sword sleep in my hand:
> Till we have built Jerusalem,
> In England's green & pleasant Land.

The oath of commitment to fulfill that potential, using all powers that are available to us. Not ceasing until it is done. Till we do have that fairer society, that Jerusalem. But, this was not rational, it does not depend on a forced idea of what that fairness is; instead, it is all about allowing that divine nature, that Life-Force, to come through and do it. Our role was one of being a willing companion. Putting all our energies into cooperating with a "friendly universe" to allow it to order our chaotic society.

This has been hugely inspirational to me. I had it sung at our wedding, and when we first arrived in America we had it sung there, too. It drove me as I went into the church. It took me through college, and then into actually working as a parish priest. Working as a priest, it was almost as if I had been prepared for the moment. I used my advertising training to publicize things. I worked again in broadcasting, writing, and presenting a series of programs about people who had had big spiritual experiences (called "Divine Encounters" on BBC Radio Kent). I organized and tried to inspire.

It was interesting how much of what I was trying to do fitted into conventional church life. That concept of a unitive experience of consciousness is so embedded in Christian theology ("The Kingdom of heaven is within you"; Moses's burning bush; Paul on the road to Damascus; the Transfiguration) that nobody turned a hair at anything I said. It helped that I had had some experience of how fundamentalists thought about these things. There is not much difference between being "born again" and having an enlightenment "peak experience," and once I realized that most of what separated the different factions within the church was actually a function of language, I was home free.

The key thing was not to "frighten the horses." There was no point in challenging strongly held beliefs because that caused problems. Instead, I steered around the beliefs and picked my battles carefully. In the end, I was able to feel completely at home in what I was communicating, without alienating the more conservative elements of the community.

When I moved to Norwich I was able to go further. I still had a vision of making a difference to the overall church, but I began to focus on creating a community of people who shared the values I held. To that end I created the Developing Consciousness Course, and subsequent book, to enable people to get an idea of the basics. When I first became interested in spirituality, I was focused on the idea of enlightenment. And yet I could find no one to give me impartial advice. Everyone wanted me to join their religion, do their form of meditation, or believe what they thought I ought to believe. "Meditate for two years and your mind will be in the right space to hear what enlightenment really is" or "come and join us, wear orange and follow our teacher and you will get enlightened." I did not want that; I wanted to know the lay of the land I was getting into. What areas should I be thinking about? Which practices worked and which did not? As a result, I subtitled the book and the course "A Roadmap of the Journey to Enlightenment."

I was not trying to say what enlightenment was, or tell anyone how to get there. I was just laying out the territory; and over fourteen years we did build a community that aspired toward these values. We brought in speakers from all over the world. We held unconventional gatherings. We performed rituals and ceremonies that were both magical and mythical, and we did everything we could to spread the ideas both within the church and outside it.

I was always asked, "Does the bishop know what you are doing?" And, of course, he did. He had no problem with it, as it all came out of a fundamental understanding of the nature of reality that was clearly in the Bible. It is just that it is not what you normally hear from the pulpit. This was Christianity as an Eastern religion, and it was also a part of the Contemplative tradition.

There was a continual struggle between "making it happen," and "allowing it to happen," between allowing the Life-Force, and forcing life, but the reality was that most of the work was done on the meditation stool. Throughout this time, I had a regular meditation practice, and it was here that the battle was fought. Holding ideas within a context of holding thoughts. Meister Eckhart says that in meditation you realize that you want for nothing, therefore you decide to will nothing, and hold the realization that fundamentally we know nothing. Wanting for nothing, willing nothing, knowing nothing. Entering that state of poverty in meditation enabled me to hold ideas without rushing forward with them.

We are always so rich in our ideas, that true poverty is often the willingness not to know, and therefore to hold all ideas equally and as Lao Tzu says:

> Do you have the patience to wait
> till your mud settles and the water is clear?
> Can you remain unmoving
> till the right action arises by itself?

During this time, my practice was the guiding light of what I was doing. I was lucky in that I had developed the practice over twenty-five years, and it was not a struggle. I did not wake up and think "I must do my meditation practice." I did it in the same way I brushed my teeth every morning. It just came naturally. But it has not always been so. I began with a practice that lasted three minutes, and have gradually added minutes to it. It now lasts an hour. But I don't do it every day, I do it five days a week, in the mornings only, and not when I am on vacation.

That gives me balance. I like having a couple of days off to do other things. I don't like evenings, and vacations are for vacating. It seems to me that everyone has their own balance, and I like to encourage people to find what is right for them.

Coming to Aspen meant a change in my vision. I still held to the ideas in Blake's poem, but I was no longer focused on the Church of England. Aspen is a unique place in that it is founded on a "Mind, Body, and Spirit" ideal, and to that end has all kinds of festivals for ideas and music, as well as being a skiing resort; and so I found my vision broaden into one of communicating ideas that could get picked up by all the various people that come through the city.

They say that "what happens in Vegas stays in Vegas." With Aspen, it is the opposite way round. "What happens in Aspen should not stay in Aspen." With all the people coming and going, Aspen is like a wormhole into different parts of America; politics, the arts, music, academia, and sport. Leaders in all these areas pass through the town, and they can take ideas out with them. The Aspen Chapel community has done every course under the sun: EST, Divine Light, TM, Mind-up, Yoga; you name it and they have done it. As a result, there is a desire to get an inclusive vision out there. A vision that includes all races, religions, wisdom, traditions, genders, and sexual orientation. One where "there are no others."

The chapel gave the possibility for that. It is rooted in the Christian tradition, but in its branches, the other religions can nest and make a contribution. Writing this book is a part of that vision. Interestingly enough, I had to weigh up forcing the material, or allowing it to come through guided by that Life-Force.

In the end, I did a bit of both. The title came over dinner with my wife. The material came naturally from speaking in the chapel; and then I would go out running with an idea, and allow it to grow and develop over the run. Not making it come, but just having a space for it to arrive.

Writing this second part of the book as a memoir, based on the six levels of consciousness, came on such a run. That to me is the essence of visionary consciousness: There is an idea out there, a problem that needs to be solved; we hold that problem, we think about it, and then out of nowhere something else comes along as an answer. There is no end to it, just a desire to have something come about and the willingness to wait for an answer, rather than force it through.

When the answer comes, then one can move into soul consciousness.

Barking Mad

2000

I had recently moved into a new house on one of the local estates at the beginning of my time as a parish priest. It was a modern terraced house. It had two bedrooms and a small box room. I decided to convert that box room into a meditation space. I painted it white and brought in my low table with candle on it, my prayer rug, and my prayer stool. It was perfect.

The next morning, I sat down to begin my first meditation in the new house.

After a few moments, I heard a bark from a dog coming right through the wall. And then another, and then another.

My meditation room was right against the house next door, and the dog was in the next room.

I struggled through what turned out to be a barking meditation.

The following morning the same thing happened. I tried earplugs. No joy.

Over the next few days I mentally fought to concentrate on my practice, trying to ignore the barking and simply focus on what I was doing.

Nothing worked. And my practice became a trial rather than the source of peace that it was supposed to be.

Then I hit on an idea; I would include the dog within my meditation, I would make the barking a part of my practice.

And it worked like a dream. I began the meditation, the dog barked and I welcomed the bark. Every time it barked, I opened myself to hearing fully the dog's contribution.

Very soon I was able to get my practice back on line. The dog was there, but so was the peace.

After a while I began not to notice the dog at all. I could just come into my space and begin meditating without any problems.

Sometime later it dawned on me that not only was I not noticing the dog, but in fact the dog was not actually making a noise. The barking had stopped and I was able to meditate in complete silence again.

A few days later I met my neighbor on the step outside and mentioned how quiet the dog had been.

"Yes," he said, "it is a strange thing, our little Johnnie seemed perfectly fine up to a couple of weeks ago. Then, quite suddenly, he just died."

Chapter 11
Coming Home

Soul Consciousness

The first time I felt an expanded awareness was when I came back from India. I felt myself as a part of a greater consciousness, and it left me with no doubt that I was a part of something far greater than myself. That experience inspired me to change careers and focus on communicating the essence of that reality. However, there was still an element of dysfunction in my life.

I was still plagued by a need and desire for love: Longing to get married or have a meaningful relationship, the need for touch, and the inability to express my emotions all continued to have an effect on the balance of my life, often leading me into dark places. I was also convinced that I had "the answer," or at least "an answer" to the problems of the world, and therefore was pretty evangelical about the self-awareness training I was involved in and the rightness of our approach to life.

This led to me driving away most of my friends and family who reacted to my sudden volte-face from a laid-back sex and drugs and rock-and-roll approach to life, to a fiery-eyed absolutist.

I can remember meeting my mother for lunch soon after this conversion, and she, instead of finding the usual sullen-faced lad, was confronted by a beaming born-again expression clutching a huge bunch of flowers and professing love for her. "Where has my son gone?" she cried.

Over that time, although I was reaching for something new and different, and I was professing a grander and more expanded vision for my life, I was still in the thrall of a desire to prove myself right in some way. The vision was there, but not a settled experience from which I could communicate peace.

That really only came when I joined the church. Not because it was latent in church life; there is enough righteousness in the church to feed any ego; but rather it was something in myself that began to change. Letting go of the effects of my emotional bankruptcy was one thing—being willing to be in pain rather than find coping strategies, but also a mellowing in the idea that I should be wanting to convert everyone else into my way of thinking.

I was painfully aware of churches' limitations, and was therefore under no illusion that "the answer" was that everyone should become a Christian, and so I began to relax into the idea that maybe if I was able to change myself, then this would bring some good to those around me. Getting married helped in that it put my emotional life on a different level, and dealt with a multitude of sins, but I also gave up trying to convert the world to my way of thinking.

In my first parish, I began working on the local estate. And there you could not be absolutist about who should be doing what. There was one particular family I used to visit. They were almost like the Gallaghers in *Shameless*. I'd turn up and there would be a roomful of people smoking dope. "Oh, it's only Nicholas the Vicar," they used to say and welcomed me in. I did not partake. One Christmas, Jim, the dad, took me to one side and confidentially told me how proud he was of his son. "You know," he said, "every year, at this time, I have to go out at night, climb over the wall of the local garden center, find a tree, haul it back over the wall and set it up at home for the family. This year, without me asking him to, young Liam went out, scaled the wall in the night and brought home this beautiful tree. I was so proud of him. From little acorns …" When I came to organize a rock festival on the estate I put Jim in charge of security.

Life became more about day-to-day living rather than any great goal or achievement, and to that end I began to let go into that Life-Force.

Meister Eckhart says that "A man should become truly poor in his life, that is to say as free from 'will' as he was when he was born. I say to you that as long as you try to fulfill the 'will of God,' or have any desire after eternity and God, you are not truly poor."

What he is really saying here is that as long as you have an agenda that you are working toward, whether that agenda is to do good or not, then the ego is still at play and that Life-Force is not really in control. It is the attachment to the agenda that he is referring to. The idea that we know what is right. Instead, we are being asked to hold ideas lightly. Put our energy into things, but not be too worried if they do not go the way we think they should.

This is why at my next parish I could settle down into the way of a local vicar. I still had ideas as to what worked and what did not work, but I was not insistent about the way they went. All the work in this area took place in my daily practice. I used to take my thoughts and worries into my meditation time and just let them go. Allowing myself not to be too fixed on things going one way or the other. Life began to flow much more naturally.

When I was in advertising, every campaign I wrote was a result of much struggle and heartache, and I often needed various "substances" to open me up to some new aspect of creativity. The trouble with that is, once you start using substances to be creative, it is very difficult to stop. When you got stuck, you remembered that the last time this happened you had a drink or a smoke or whatever, and so you do it again. Very soon you simply cannot create without that substance. This is why the creative industries are often plagued with a drug problem.

I had to write a sermon every week, and I found that they came very easily through my practice. I did not have to strain it out, it just came. And so, over those years, I began to develop an ease in my life, which was very different to how I had worked in the past. Gone was the fast life of advertising, and gone was the evangelical certainty. Instead, there was more of a flow that came from a sense of peace. "The trouble with you," one senior church leader told me, "is that you are contented." I quite liked the accusation.

When it came time for me to write my first book, we went as a family to America. I wrote 1,700 words in the morning, and 1,700 words in the afternoon, while my wife took the kids out to museums. Finding a publisher was a lot more difficult than writing the book. But with children, family, work, and all sorts of things, life inevitably throws up problems, and again, when that happened I took them into my practice.

I would take an experience of distress and work with it. Turning it over, trying not to push it away. Trying to change myself rather than the circumstances. And that brought a new depth to my understanding of the way that life worked.

It also brought me to look at death more clearly. Because every "letting go" is, in fact, a mini death. You begin to face something and realize that you cannot change it, and it becomes like something you must die to. So, inevitably, you begin to think about your own death.

No matter how enlightened we are, how steeped in Christ, how flowing with the Tao, how in touch with our Buddha nature, how realized our consciousness, unless we have reconciled ourselves with death we are still living in an idealized fabricated reality that is in some way driven by the narcissistic nature of our ego; and I am not talking about reconciling ourselves to going to heaven or hell, or buying into one traditional concept or other which may or may not be true. I am talking about recognizing our own mortality, and the fact that we will cease to exist.

And yet we do not really want to confront death.

We push it out to the edge of our consciousness. We are aware of it. We make our wills, we might even give some thought to our memorials—but only in a joking way: "Make sure you have that tune when I die!" But I think maturity and peace comes from having death front and center in our lives.

Aspen is notorious for trying to put off death. Keeping fit, trying to look and be young, our appearance. All of that is OK, unless it is an attempt to push away the inevitability of death. Maturity is having death with us at every step of the way; and not just the death of our bodies, but also the death of our ideas and our plans. Our friends and our family. Our fitness and our capability.

We have to continually live with the impermanence of everything. And I think that is the nature of real maturity.

Rumi wrote the poem "Rebirth":

> I died as a mineral and became a plant
> I died as a plant and rose to animal
> I died as animal and I was human.
> Why should I fear? When was I less by dying?
> Yet once more I shall die as human to soar
> With angels blest. But even from an angel
> I must pass on: all except God must perish.
> When I have sacrificed my angel soul,
> I shall become what no mind ever conceived.[2]

The maturity that comes with a moment-by-moment companionship with death is the maturity of surrender.

As Richard Rohr says:

> Surrendering to the divine Flow is not about giving up, giving in, capitulating, becoming a puppet, being naïve, being irresponsible, or stopping all planning and thinking.
>
> Surrender is about a peaceful inner opening that keeps the conduit of living water flowing.
>
> It is a quiet willingness to trust that you really are a beloved son or a beloved daughter, which allows

God to be your Father and Mother. It really is that simple, which for the human ego is very hard.[3]

You can see it in Jesus's life. His life was about that surrender. He walked with death throughout his ministry. He knew that the journey was to Jerusalem and he lived with the idea that his death was going to be as important as his life—which it proved to be. "If it is possible, let this cup of suffering be taken away from me. Yet may thy will to be done, not mine."

To live in the companionship of death is to live with the ongoing realization that everything that we see, feel, touch, and relate to is subject to change. That life as we know it, in all its forms, can and will change irrevocably, and that we need be constantly aware of that in all that we do.

Such a realization brings real maturity. The maturity that does not try to hold on to what we have, but is willing to let it go. The knowledge that we can be reconciled to the possibilities in our past, and the possibilities in our future, and be at peace with both. That is what it is to live in soul consciousness.

In that consciousness, the ego (to the extent that it can) is continually bowing to the possibility of death, and surrendering to the divine. That is the place of maturity, because it shows full and unreserved cooperation with the unfolding of life.

And it impacts in many different ways. To begin with, we stop desperately holding on ... to anything, our jobs, our plans, our relationships; we hold them lightly, and therefore more lovingly. We start to let go of control. After all, we are not in control anyway, so the idea that we can control life is really just an illusion. To live with death is to live in the present, to deal with what is, rather than what might be.

And, of course, there is our own physical demise. We must live with that, too, which is why I bring my death into my daily meditation. How do I feel about it? What do I think about my dying? What does it mean to me to know that I will no longer be here, and that I don't really know what will happen next? What about my family? How will my death impact them?

To live with death is to have it be a constant companion in all that we do. Not pushing it away. Not trying to disguise the signs of its presence; and that relationship with the impermanence brings us to a mature attitude to life. It enables us to live fully and equally in multiple contexts. To hold paradoxes, and not to feel that we have to be right about everything. To welcome change, to let go, and to truly dance.

I think the idea of walking or dancing with death takes practice, which is why I think it is good to bring it into our daily practices; however, it is also something that we have to continually keep in our minds. Like walking a labyrinth, our lives twist and turn, and unless we can twist and turn with that flow of life, we become stuck. When we hold onto things lightly, we do not become stuck, because we are always letting go into the next phase. There is no stuckness, there is just surrender to what is; and so I have come to a stage in my life where I have begun to feel a sense of equanimity about what happens. Even with this book. As Lao Tzu says:

> Do your work, then step back.
> The only path to serenity.

The same goes for my work at the Aspen Chapel, my family life, money, and the future. There is nothing much I can constructively do about any of it. Yes, I still have ideas, and I work hard to bring them about, but I hope I am not too attached to the outcome. They say that an expectation is an upset waiting to happen, and a disappointment is one that did. And that sums it up. I do not know what difference I will make to anything; that is not up to me. Like the story of that nurse in *Romeo and Juliet*, the temptation is for me to see myself as the star of my own movie. But in reality, I am a bit player in a sideshow put on for an audience that I am unaware of.

That is what it means to live for the Life-Force. It is not really our life or our agenda. To acknowledge that is to arrive at a point of sanity. And that means you can truly live the life that you were meant to.

As George Eliot once said, "It is never too late to become the person you might have been."

Appendix

From *Developing Consciousness: A Roadmap of the Journey to Enlightenment*

1979 aged 25—"I can tell you what's going on—But that might not tell you what is going on."

I had never really been interested in "spirituality."

It seemed somehow fey, in the excessively refined sense of the word. Not something that could deal with the slings and arrows that I felt coming my way in real life.

That changed on a trip to the Himalayas. I suddenly got the sense that there might be a way through: That the other worldliness which I had glimpsed on the side of the mountain might be able to take me out of my daily pain management.

Maybe sex and drugs and rock and roll weren't the long-term solution.

I came back from India with an idea that there might be some value in it; hence my still wearing Indian clothes and going vegetarian.

I had one lead. A friend of mine had "got religion" of the Indian kind and sold all his possessions to visit his guru in India. I had benefited to the tune of two huge Ditton 15 speakers that I picked up for a song from him.

He was back now and I went to visit him in his farmhouse near Bristol.

"Right, yeah," he said, "what do you want to know?"

"Well, er, what is it all about? Where do you start?"

"You are in everything, and everything is in you."

"What?"

"You are in everything, and everything is in you."

This was going to be hard.

I explained that this was not much help and he shrugged his shoulders enigmatically and said, "Well, you could always read Paramahansa Yogananda's Autobiography of a Yogi.*"*

He had a copy to hand and I removed myself from his presence and went home to be enlightened.

I devoured it—page by page, word by word.

It didn't tell me much about me, but it told me all about him. And the thing that came across is that he "knew." Shot through as it was with quirky tales of gurus, non-eating saints, and all sorts of jiggery pockery, what rang true was that there was another dimension to life that was accessible. He had experienced it; I wanted to experience it too.

At the back of the book was an address in California that would send you lessons in something called Kriya Yoga. Send $25 and they would send you the lessons by sea mail.

I sent them $50 and told them to send it by air.

Within days I was sitting on an upright chair in my bedroom focusing on "a place between your eyes" and breathing deeply.

Nothing much happened. It might be because, although I had temporarily given up tobacco as a nod to my new spiritual quest, I was still out every evening in clubs or at parties, so my meditation had to be in the morning after I got up and before I went to work, which would be about 10:30 a.m.

I soon got bored. However, I was still very much on the spiritual trail.

I read everything I could get hold of. I did courses and self-awareness seminars. I meditated before going to work, and I tried to pick up the more spiritual girls that I came across.

After a while I came to the conclusion that there was such a thing as enlightenment, and again, I wanted it.

Amazingly, I had the experience that I was looking for.

I had been on the spiritual search for all of seven months, and it happened.

Before I tell you what actually did happen, I want to say that I know it will sound trite. But there really is no way to adequately express the inexpressible.

Whatever you say will sound unremarkable.

"Well ... I was sitting under this tree ... I think it was a banyan when suddenly ..."

You try it.

I also want to say that I do not think that the experience that I had was "the" experience, in the sense that it is the experience that everyone has to have to "get enlightened."

It was just the experience I had that moved me on from thinking of myself as an individual living my own separate life in this big wide world, to realizing that I was a part of something bigger.

Finally, one more codicil to the description I am about to give you.

There is a famous scene in the film Solaris *(George Clooney's version) where George's character asks one of the engineers on the space station, "What's going on here?"*

The engineer replies, "I can tell you what's going on; but that might not tell you what is going on." The same applies here.

I am going to tell you the experience that I had, but it still might mean absolutely nothing to you.

I was sitting in a room with a group of friends one evening. Not my house, someone else's. We were listening to some music; Lowell George, I think.

Someone asked me if I played the guitar. I did not.

"Well," they said, "why not try listening to the music and see if you can play along with it."

When I reflected on it afterward the conclusion I came to was that, somehow, I had focused on this music in such a way that it shut out all my other senses, and as a result I was able to get beyond my mind's insistence as to what was real and what was not real, and so this new dimension was able to open up to me.

What actually happened was that my perception of the nature of reality shifted dramatically.

Whereas normally I look out and I see people, in a space that is contained by the periphery of my vision, suddenly I felt myself to be a part of something infinitely greater than myself. It was as if I was a glove puppet, and there was something hugely vast that was both containing me and everything around me.

And I suddenly understood what it meant to "see the light."

Not some ethereal understanding, but actual light.

This "light" was coming from somewhere behind me, in my consciousness, and it manifested in tiny optical fibers that came through me. I was seeing those fibers as they came through my eyes and connected with everything I saw in front of me, in the room.

Everything was made of light. That light came through my consciousness, created all that I saw in front of me, and then seemed to disappear into infinity.

I was a part of something much bigger than myself. Whatever it was, it was creating me and allowing me to see my connection, through those optical fibers, with everything else in the room.

Two things struck me.

First, that all things were interconnected; not just in the sense that all things relate together, but also in that this light seemed to be a vehicle through which all this was manifesting.

Second, there was a "greater being"; something was holding this together. There was a fundamental order to life. I was a part of that order, and so was everything I was looking at.

In an instant I recognized the experience as exactly fitting the descriptions of enlightenment that I had read about. I understood what my friend had meant when he said, "you are in everything, and everything is in you."

Suddenly everything went "clunk-click," and I knew that this is what I had been wanting to experience.

No one else in the room saw anything. I said, "WOW" a few times, and tried to explain what I was seeing, but it did not hold much interest.

All in all the experience lasted about three hours.

I went home and just sat and stared into space.

I did not emerge from my flat for three days, but when I did I saw everything in a different light. It was as if I had seen "Outside" for the first time.

It was true. It existed.

I was amazed that people seemed to be going about their lives, not knowing the full nature of the reality of the life that they were living.

Newsreaders made no reference to this interconnectedness. In fact, everyone lived their lives as if they were completely separate from each other, as I had done only a few days before.

I was faced with a dilemma: What was I to do about it?

It was as if I had been invited to a drinks party at 10 Downing Street.

Halfway through the evening I needed to pee, so went to the loo.

I opened the door, and there sitting on the loo was the prime minister. Not only was he sitting on the loo, but his head was resting somewhere by his feet, and where his head should have been, there was the head of an alien monster.

Stunned, I closed the door; the prime minister was an alien. What's more I knew that the prime minister was an alien.

I was faced with a choice. Did I go out into the party and say, "Hey guys, guess what, the prime minister is an alien," and have everyone think I was completely bonkers; or did I carry on with my life and just pretend that it had not happened?

That was my dilemma now.

Did I tell everyone what I had seen ("lock him up quick before he does any damage to himself, or to us"), or did I think of it as an aberration and try to forget it?

I did try to forget it. I forced myself to go out and see everything as being separate, but I never got further than the end of the road. It just fitted so perfectly. It just made sense. And so gradually I accepted it. I came to the conclusion that, for whatever reason, I had been given a glimpse into something. Not only that, but I was in a place where that understanding of the nature of reality was not common knowledge.

I almost felt that it was my duty to communicate what I had seen.

I was working in advertising at the time, so a few days later I walked into Saatchi and Saatchi and resigned.

They thought I was mad. I probably was.

Managing director Ron Legas asked to see me.

"It has taken you three years to get this job. We have just won the general election and Mrs. Thatcher is in power, do you really want to throw it all away for some whim? You'll regret it."

In the end I did walk, and to this day I have never regretted it.

I have never had the same experience again, but every day I see echoes of it in the way that life works.

In the beauty that is all around me.

In the way that human beings treat each other.

In the violence that comes from not understanding our true nature, and what we mean to each other.

And in the way that life works itself out in each of us.

Notes

Chapter 1

1. From "In Memoriam" (London: Edward Moxom, 1850).
2. Albert Einstein, quoted at www.nlpu.com/Articles/Sept_11.html.
3. T. S. Eliot, *Four Quartets* (Harcourt, 1943).
4. Philip K. Dick, "How to Build a Universe That Doesn't Fall Apart Two Days Later," *The Shifting Realities of Philip K. Dick: Selected Literary and Philosophical Writings*, 1995.

Chapter 2

1. William Shakespeare, from Hamlet, Act 3 Scene 1.
2. Stephen Mitchell, trans., *Tao Te Ching No 61* (New York: Harper and Row, 1988).
3. Eknath Easwaran, trans., *The Dhammapada No 19* (The Blue Mountain Center of Meditation, 1985).
4. Stephen Mitchell, trans., *Tao Te Ching No 7* (New York: Harper and Row, 1988).
5. Holy Bible, New International Version. Genesis 2:17.
6. Aldous Huxley, *The Perennial Philosophy* (Triad Grafton, 1989), 9.
7. Stephen Mitchell, trans., *Tao Te Ching No 15* (New York: Harper and Row 1988).
8. Khalil Gibran, *The Prophet* (Pan Books, 1991), 70.
9. Holy Bible, New International Version. Matthew 16:26.
10. Jellaludin Rumi, translation by Coleman Barks.
11. Holy Bible, King James Version. Matthew 28–29.

Chapter 3

1. Khalil Gibran, *The Prophet* (Pan Books, 1991), 70.
2. Albert Einstein, quoted at www.nlpu.com/Articles/Sept_11.html.
3. Holy Bible, New International Version.

Chapter 4

1. Swami Prabhavananda, *The Upanishads*, trans. Frederick Manchester (Vedanta Press, 1975), 165.
2. Bede Griffiths, *Return to the Centre* (Fount, 1978), 74.
3. T. S. Eliot, *Four Quartets* (Harcourt, 1943).

Chapter 6

1. William Blake, from the preface to *Milton*, 1808.

Chapter 7

2. Rumi, *The Essential Rumi* (San Francisco: Harper, 1995).

Chapter 8

3. Richard Rohr, Daily Meditations, "You Are Not in Control," Thursday, May 26, 2016.

About the Author

Nicholas was brought up in England before moving to America in 2014 to serve in a community in Colorado.

He trod the traditional path of a writer; beginning in broadcasting and then moving to advertising before meeting his Waterloo on the slopes of the Himalayas in the form of an experience of 'altered consciousness'.

Since then he has been exploring ways to live life more skillfully - making sense of what is, what should be and what could be.

He is the Author of: "Developing Consciousness – A roadmap of the Journey to Enlightenment".

Books by Nicholas Vesey

Living the Life-Force
Published by: Ozark Mountain Publishing

Developing Consciousness: A Road Map of the Journey to
Enlightenment
Published by: John Hunt Publishing

For more information about any of the above titles, soon to be released titles,
or other items in our catalog, write, phone or visit our website:
Ozark Mountain Publishing, Inc.
PO Box 754, Huntsville, AR 72740
479-738-2348/800-935-0045
www.ozarkmt.com

If you liked this book, you might also like:

Heaven Here on Earth
by Curt Melliger
Waking Up in the Spiritual Age
by Dr. Dan Bird
We are the Creators
by L.R. Sumpter
Imagining the Unimaginable
by Richard Rowe
Akashic Records: One True Love
by Gabrielle Orr
And Then I Knew My Abundance
by James Nussbaumer

For more information about any of the above titles, soon to be released titles,
or other items in our catalog, write, phone or visit our website:
Ozark Mountain Publishing, Inc.
PO Box 754, Huntsville, AR 72740
479-738-2348
www.ozarkmt.com

For more information about any of the titles published by Ozark Mountain Publishing, Inc., soon to be released titles, or other items in our catalog, write, phone or visit our website:

Ozark Mountain Publishing, Inc.

PO Box 754

Huntsville, AR 72740

479-738-2348/800-935-0045

www.ozarkmt.com

Other Books by Ozark Mountain Publishing, Inc.

Dolores Cannon
A Soul Remembers Hiroshima
Between Death and Life
Conversations with Nostradamus,
    Volume I, II, III
The Convoluted Universe -Book One,
    Two, Three, Four, Five
The Custodians
Five Lives Remembered
Jesus and the Essenes
Keepers of the Garden
Legacy from the Stars
The Legend of Starcrash
The Search for Hidden Sacred Knowledge
They Walked with Jesus
The Three Waves of Volunteers and the
    New Earth
Aron Abrahamsen
Holiday in Heaven
Out of the Archives – Earth Changes
Justine Alessi & M. E. McMillan
Rebirth of the Oracle
Kathryn/Patrick Andries
Naked in Public
Kathryn Andries
The Big Desire
Dream Doctor
Soul Choices: Six Paths to Find Your Life
    Purpose
Soul Choices: Six Paths to Fulfilling
    Relationships
Patrick Andries
Owners Manual for the Mind
Dan Bird
Finding Your Way in the Spiritual Age
Waking Up in the Spiritual Age
Julia Cannon
Soul Speak – The Language of Your Body
Ronald Chapman
Seeing True
Albert Cheung
The Emperor's Stargate
Jack Churchward
Lifting the Veil on the Lost Continent of
    Mu
The Stone Tablets of Mu
Sherri Cortland
Guide Group Fridays
Raising Our Vibrations for the New Age

Spiritual Tool Box
Windows of Opportunity
Patrick De Haan
The Alien Handbook
Paulinne Delcour-Min
Spiritual Gold
Michael Dennis
Morning Coffee with God
God's Many Mansions
Carolyn Greer Daly
Opening to Fullness of Spirit
Anita Holmes
Twidders
Aaron Hoopes
Reconnecting to the Earth
Victoria Hunt
Kiss the Wind
Patricia Irvine
In Light and In Shade
Kevin Killen
Ghosts and Me
Diane Lewis
From Psychic to Soul
Donna Lynn
From Fear to Love
Maureen McGill
Baby It's You
Maureen McGill & Nola Davis
Live from the Other Side
Curt Melliger
Heaven Here on Earth
Henry Michaelson
And Jesus Said – A Conversation
Dennis Milner
Kosmos
Andy Myers
Not Your Average Angel Book
Guy Needler
Avoiding Karma
Beyond the Source – Book 1, Book 2
The Anne Dialogues
The Curators
The History of God
The Origin Speaks
James Nussbaumer
And Then I Knew My Abundance
The Master of Everything
Mastering Your Own Spiritual Freedom

For more information about any of the above titles, soon to be released titles,
or other items in our catalog, write, phone or visit our website:
PO Box 754, Huntsville, AR 72740
479-738-2348/800-935-0045
www.ozarkmt.com

Other Books by Ozark Mountain Publishing, Inc.

Sherry O'Brian
Peaks and Valleys
Riet Okken
The Liberating Power of Emotions
Gabrielle Orr
Akashic Records: One True Love
Let Miracles Happen
Victor Parachin
Sit a Bit
Nikki Pattillo
A Spiritual Evolution
Children of the Stars
Rev. Grant H. Pealer
A Funny Thing Happened on the
    Way to Heaven
Worlds Beyond Death
Victoria Pendragon
Born Healers
Feng Shui from the Inside, Out
Sleep Magic
The Sleeping Phoenix
Michael Perlin
Fantastic Adventures in Metaphysics
Walter Pullen
Evolution of the Spirit
Debra Rayburn
Let's Get Natural with Herbs
Charmian Redwood
A New Earth Rising
Coming Home to Lemuria
David Rivinus
Always Dreaming
Richard Rowe
Imagining the Unimaginable
M. Don Schorn
Elder Gods of Antiquity
Legacy of the Elder Gods
Gardens of the Elder Gods
Reincarnation...Stepping Stones of Life
Garnet Schulhauser
Dance of Eternal Rapture
Dance of Heavenly Bliss

Dancing Forever with Spirit
Dancing on a Stamp
Manuella Stoerzer
Headless Chicken
Annie Stillwater Gray
Education of a Guardian Angel
The Dawn Book
Work of a Guardian Angel
Blair Styra
Don't Change the Channel
Who Catharted
Natalie Sudman
Application of Impossible Things
L.R. Sumpter
Judy's Story
The Old is New
We Are the Creators
Jim Thomas
Tales from the Trance
Nicholas Vesey
Living the Life-Force
Janie Wells
Embracing the Human Journey
Payment for Passage
Dennis Wheatley/ Maria Wheatley
The Essential Dowsing Guide
Maria Wheatley
Druidic Soul Star Astrology
Jacquelyn Wiersma
The Zodiac Recipe
Sherry Wilde
The Forgotten Promise
Lyn Willmoth
A Small Book of Comfort
Stuart Wilson & Joanna Prentis
Atlantis and the New Consciousness
Beyond Limitations
The Essenes -Children of the Light
The Magdalene Version
Power of the Magdalene
Robert Winterhalter
The Healing Christ

For more information about any of the above titles, soon to be released titles,
or other items in our catalog, write, phone or visit our website:
PO Box 754, Huntsville, AR 72740
479-738-2348/800-935-0045
www.ozarkmt.com